The Marketing Almanac

Michelle Pontes

Dear Lottie!
I hope this book brings you valuable insights and inspiration.
Michelle

ISBN: 9798321701409

Independently published.

DEDICATION

To Limoni and Matilda.
As I sit down to write this little note in my book, I can't help but think of the two of you, my beautiful girls, and all the meaning you bring to my life. This book might seem like it's just about marketing, but between these lines there's a journey, a before and an after.
So, it's your journey too, in a way.
It's a reminder that there's no dream too big. Believe in your own strength, your own worth, as fiercely as I believe in you.
Love always,

Mama

Table of Contents

ACKNOWLEDGMENTS

Writing "The Marketing Almanac" has been a journey of self-discovery, and a culmination of countless hours of dedication and passion. I've been fortunate to be surrounded by individuals whose support was indispensable.

To Tom, what can I say? You are a steadfast presence whose voice always resonates with encouragement, pushing me to explore beyond the comfortable and the known. Your belief in me, often stronger than my own, has propelled me to take leaps of faith, to trust in my journey, and to find my own voice.

Artur, your pragmatism, and directness are a rare and invaluable trait. Ambiguity often clouds judgment, your clear, no-nonsense advice cut through the fog offering me the simple answers I needed.

Camilla, your attention to detail and thoughtful suggestions have enriched this book in countless ways.

Lastly, to Stef, who always brings a personal touch to everything you do. Your ideas, drenched in experience and empathy, have left an imprint, and this book is all the richer for it.

To each of you, thank you.

INTRODUCTION

The comfort of taking notes

I have always found comfort in the simple act of taking notes. My life is a collection of experiences lived across Europe: from the serene beauty of Funchal to the agitation of London, passing through Lisbon, Porto, Amsterdam, Brussels, and Geneva. In every place, my professional career has somehow been documented in countless notebooks, on post-its, and scribbles on loose pages.

I am, undeniably, a "serial" note-taker. My thoughts, learnings, and ideas have found a home on piles of paper, each note a breadcrumb on the path of my career.

The idea for this Marketing Almanac started from these fragments of creativity. It dawned on me (or rather, a good friend suggested) that within these scattered pages lay the blueprint for an innovative marketing book. This moment of realisation connected the dots between a personal habit and a professional resource, showing the potential of my notes to serve a greater purpose. The Marketing Almanac is a compilation of notes and an embodiment of my journey as a marketer, a strategist and a planner who has experienced the complexities of business across cultural and geographic boundaries.

The intention behind this almanac is simple yet ambitious. I want to give you concise and practical advice that you can apply each month of the year. So, why not give it a try?

Whether you are a seasoned marketer or just starting, this almanac is intended to inspire and provoke thought. It is an ideal gift for business starters and leaders, offering a comprehensive view of the marketing function's full scope. Marketing is not a job for a solitary figure; it demands a varied and adept skill set to truly resonate. This point is exemplified throughout the almanac, encouraging teamwork and the sharing of diverse perspectives.

The concept

Someone once told me, "teach them the what, not the how". This piece of advice has profoundly shaped my approach to marketing, business, management and even how I raise my children. By focusing on the outcomes, the "what" we aim to achieve, we open the door to creative exploration, encouraging critical thinking and problem-solving skills. This philosophy is the cornerstone of this almanac, explicitly guiding its structure and content. For instance, each section is designed to highlight key marketing outcomes, followed by examples, and thought exercises that encourage you, the reader, to discover your own pathway to these outcomes, consequently integrating this advice into the very fabric of the almanac.

Aligning this almanac to the financial year was a deliberate choice. It sets the rhythm for business planning and financial forecasting, giving a more organised and strategic approach to marketing and business development. For example, a chapter dedicated to strategic planning at the start of the financial year can help readers apply the almanac's insights in real-time, making this alignment a practical tool for businesses and individuals alike. However, understanding the universality of businesses across the globe, the months within this almanac are marked as "month one," "month two," and so on, ensuring its accessibility and relevance regardless of geographical location or financial calendar.

The almanac gives you useful suggestions and insights each month. You'll discover a carefully selected monthly marketing book suggestion to broaden your understanding and spark your creativity. Read a new book every month, refresh or acquire new marketing skills, and I guarantee you, by the end of Month 12, you'll be in a far better place than where you started. And there's more. Every month includes marketing actions and suggestions to help you seize the unique opportunities of that specific month. I mean practical, relevant guidance that you can use in real life.

Each month's content also includes sustainable marketing tips. As marketers, I believe it's our responsibility to pursue our goals with sustainability as a priority. This section will help you select planet- friendly alternatives in your marketing activities, ensuring that your success contributes to a healthier planet.

Next, we'll discuss the future - generative AI. This technology is transforming marketing and how we executive marketing functions, so I've added a generative AI cheat sheet for each month. These cheat sheets have prompts specially made to help marketers with their tasks. In addition, I've created a monthly suggestion on how to create prompts for complex or nuanced tasks. Whether you're writing copy, studying data, or coming up with campaign ideas, AI can be your assistant, and this almanac teaches you how. Another important aspect is personal branding. In the modern online world, it's a good idea to develop and maintain your personal brand. Each month, I'll provide you with advice and actions to enhance your personal brand, so you can stand out and succeed in your area of expertise.

There's more to this book than the monthly guidance. At the end of the book, you'll find a bonus section that's as useful as the main content. Here, I cover 20 types of marketing, showing the variety and complexity of the field. You'll also see sections on marketing scope, marketing foundations, key marketing metrics, marketing lifecycles, how to create an effective marketing plan, a complete marketing toolkit, tips on event marketing, and a glossary to explain marketing terms.

Sometimes, you may think that the content of this almanac repeats itself, but that's what good marketing is all about, repeating, iterating, and pivoting. So, during the year, you should go back to previous actions and take practical steps to ensure your marketing strategy is still valid and on track.

The journey

Undertaking this project has been one of the most interesting personal projects of my life. Sifting through my notes was not only an exercise in content compilation but also an incredible journey of self-discovery. I have learned and revisited ideas, not just about marketing, but about the adaptability of the human spirit in the face of constant change. The process of creating the almanac, with its challenges of distilling vast amounts of information into coherent and useful insights, taught me the importance of perseverance, creativity, and the willingness to view old ideas through new lenses.

I hope that you, the reader, enjoy this almanac as much as I have enjoyed creating it, and encourage a fresh perspective on marketing strategies. Most importantly, I welcome your thoughts, feedback, and suggestions for next year's edition, for the journey of learning and growth never truly ends.

Michelle Pontes

MONTH 1

Must-read: **The green marketing manifesto"** by John Grant

Focus: sustainable marketing practices and eco-friendly business strategies.

SETTING THE STAGE

Month 1 is the beginning of the financial year. It's the time for businesses to set goals, allocate budgets, and strategies for the upcoming year. It's also the time for reflection on past performances and for looking forward with renewed energy and focus.

Planning at the start of the financial year is crucial. It sets the tone and direction for the months ahead. Effective planning involves understanding market trends, evaluating past performance, and setting realistic but challenging targets. Now is also the time to innovate and think creatively about tackling new markets or improving products and services.

One of the most critical aspects of financial year planning is budget allocation. Organisations must balance between investing in growth opportunities and maintaining operational efficiency. It's important to allocate funds not just based on past expenditures, but also on future growth areas.

1 - The review
Start by taking a good look at what you've achieved (or missed) in the past year. What worked? What didn't? And most importantly, why?

2 - The alignment
Align your marketing objectives with the broader business goals. You're not operating in a silo; you are part of a larger narrative. Your marketing strategies should propel the entire organisation forward, not just your own metrics.

GOOD TO KNOW
This time of the year is perfect for advocating for the resources you need. Budget discussions are on the table, and by showing how your marketing efforts contribute to the overall success, you can secure the investment required to turn your plans into reality. When asking for (more) money, be prepared to demonstrate the value you'll bring to every penny spent.

CTA: conducting a SWOT analysis is your first order of business.

SUSTAINABLE MARKETING: GOALS

The health of our planet is as important as the success of our businesses is, of course, a nonsense statement. The health of our planet is the single most important factor for human existence. Sustainability has shifted from being a niche interest to a strategy embedded in everything we do in marketing. Month 1 presents a unique opportunity for businesses to align their financial aspirations with environmental stewardship.

1 - Setting sustainable marketing goals
Evaluate past performance: Look back at the previous year's efforts and assess their environmental impact. What worked well? What improvements can be made?

Define sustainability objectives: Set clear, measurable goals that align your marketing efforts with environmental sustainability. These might include reducing the carbon footprint of your campaigns, increasing the use of recycled materials, or promoting eco-friendly products more effectively.

Communicate your brand's sustainability efforts: Make sure your brand messaging shows a dedication to sustainability, appealing to the increasing number of consumers who care about environmental responsibility.

2 - Aligning the community
Educational content: Create and share content that educates your audience about environmental issues and how your products or services offer solutions. This could include blog posts, social media content, webinars, or even in-store workshops.

Partnerships: Partner with environmental organisations or other businesses committed to sustainability. Joint initiatives can amplify your message and broaden your impact.

To-do: Align month 1 marketing with sustainability goals.

GENERATIVE AI CHEAT SHEET: FINANCIAL YEAR

We already discussed how Month 1 marks the beginning of the financial year, an important month for marketers. Generative AI emerges as an invaluable tool, offering AI-powered assistance that can transform how marketers approach their tasks.

Utilise Generative AI to generate compelling content around financial planning and budgeting tools. This not only highlights the importance of meticulous financial year planning but also positions your services as indispensable for businesses aiming for strategic growth and efficiency.

Here's two specific ways Generative AI can be leveraged this month to enhance marketing strategies.

Prompt 1: "Detail the key strategies for effective financial year planning and budget optimisation."
Application: Develop content that showcases your services or products, encouraging businesses to strategize wisely.

Prompt 2: "Highlight the benefits of attending financial year kick-off events."
Application: Promote kick-off events, emphasising networking and strategic alignment opportunities.

Refine your prompting skills.
Apply conditional logic. Use if-then statements to control ChatGPT's responses. This can help with programming or troubleshooting prompts, where you might outline situations and expected results.

PERSONAL BRAND: SELF-ASSESSMENT

Starting the journey of personal branding feels a lot like beginning a deep conversation with yourself. The initial stage of this journey, rich in introspection and self-discovery, focuses on self-assessment and goal setting - an important foundation for any enduring personal brand. Imagine your personal brand as a distinct entity - your strengths, your passions, your values.

The process begins with a deep dive into the essence of what your personal brand is about. So, where do you start? First, think about your strengths. Then, your passions. This is where you think about what you love doing. What are the things that you can talk about for hours without getting bored? And do these passions play into your brand image? Finally, your values. They are the core of your personal brand, the standards you uphold in any situation. Whether it's honesty, creativity, or resilience, your values are the rules that influence how you act and choose. They are what make people believe you and want to follow you on your professional path.

self-reflection (understand your unique blend)
passion pursuit (identify what fuels you)
value articulation (define your core principles)
goal setting (specific, measurable, achievable, relevant, and time-bound)
reality check (conduct a personal SWOT analysis)
action plan (define your core principles
review (keep your brand in check)

Week 1: Discover your unique value proposition.
The first week is dedicated to discovering and defining your unique value proposition (UVP). This involves identifying what sets you apart from others in your field, your unique skills, experiences, and the unique value you provide to your audience.

Week 2: Where do you see your brand in the future?
With a clear UVP, the second week focuses on setting goals and establishing a vision for your personal brand. This is about looking forward, envisioning where you want your brand to be.

Week 3: Understanding who they are and what they need.
Understanding your target audience is critical to the success of your personal brand. Explore where they spend their time online, the type of content they engage with, and what they seek in a brand like yours.

Week 4: Write a compelling introduction.
The last week of month 1 ends with writing a persuasive personal brand statement. This statement briefly expresses your identity, your work, your audience, and your distinctive value. A good brand statement will make you unforgettable and help you differentiate yourself in your field.

Defining your UVP, setting clear goals, understanding your audience, and creating a compelling brand statement will equip you to build a strong personal brand throughout the year.

MONTH 2

Must-read: **"Influence: the psychology of persuasion"** by Robert B. Cialdini

Focus: use the ideas of growth to learn how to persuade and influence customers in an ethical way.

INSIGHTS AND RESEARCH

Month 2 is ideal for discovering the market's psychology and understanding the essential needs of our audience. It's a time to focus on collecting and analysing customer data and market trends, basically learning about the consumer context.

Knowing your target market in this detailed way is both useful and necessary for effective marketing strategies that connect with your audience on an individual level. The goal is to close the distance between your products or services and the real needs of your clients, making sure your marketing efforts are always on target.

1 - The data

Focus on real-time data and feedback available through social media, web analytics, surveys, focus-groups, etc. These platforms offer a live wire into the current sentiment and behaviour patterns of your target audience, allowing for agile adjustments and informed decision- making.

2 - The trends

Using customer feedback from last year as a key part of your research can give you important insights into the changing wants and actions of your market. It's a practice of hearing, studying, and adjusting, giving you a strong foundation to grow your knowledge.

GOOD TO KNOW

Customer feedback from last year is a veritable treasure trove of insights. It's easy to get caught up in chasing new data, but don't overlook what you already have. Previous feedback can shed light on patterns and preferences that are still relevant. Think of it as a compass guiding your research efforts.

CTA: Engage directly with your audience through surveys, focus groups, and other market analysis trends.

SUSTAINABLE MARKETING: COMMUNITY

This month you can demonstrate your commitment to sustainability through community engagement. Businesses should align their marketing strategies to initiatives that benefit the environment and strengthen community bonds. This period is an opportunity to demonstrate how a brand's commitment to sustainability goes beyond products and services to include a broader ecological and social responsibility.

1 - Community engagement
Participate in local events: Get involved in or sponsor local community events.

Host educational workshops: organise workshops or seminars on topics related to biodiversity and sustainability. These could include talks, sustainable practices, or how to reduce one's carbon footprint.

Collaborate with local schools: Partner with local schools to educate children about biodiversity and the environment.

To-do: Create an action-plan for community engagement.

GENERATIVE AI CHEAT SHEET: GROWTH STRATEGIES

It's time to push forward with innovative growth strategies and exciting product launches, making the most of industry conferences and networking events.

Utilise Generative AI to create compelling narratives around innovative growth strategies. Highlight how participation in promotions and industry conferences can serve as catalysts for this growth. Focus on creating content that not only informs but also inspires marketers to leverage these opportunities for networking, learning, and expanding their business footprint.

Prompt 1: "Discuss innovative growth strategies for organisations this month."
Application: Create engaging content about growth tactics and how attending events and industry conferences can fuel this growth.

Prompt 2: "Share insights on launching new products successfully in a competitive market."
Application: Provide case studies or guidelines for successful product or service launches, aligning with this month's themes and opportunities.

Refine your prompting skills.
Indicate preferred level of detail: Let ChatGPT know if you want a short summary, a thorough description, or a procedural guide. This helps adjust the amount and complexity of ChatGPT's responses.

PERSONAL BRAND: YOUR NICHE

The second chapter of your personal branding journey is the point where clarity meets purpose. It's where your unique blend of talents, passions, values, and purpose meets the needs of a specific audience, a place where you're listened to and sought after.

Finding your niche is like finding your home in the professional world. A place where your strengths are recognised, and where your voice resonates with the right audience.

How do you find this sweet spot? It starts with understanding that your niche is where your story, the authentic narrative of your professional journey, intersects with a need or gap in the market. However, to find that story, you need to first understand the picture, the landscape of your industry, its trends, its gaps, and its unmet needs.

Where do you look?

Talk to industry peers, participate in forums and discussions, keep up with industry publications, and listen. Listen not just to what's being said, but to what's not being said. Pay attention to the needs that are yet to be voiced. This is where your unique value, the strengths, passions, and values you identified in the first month, begin to find its stage.

Once you start seeing patterns, gaps, and opportunities, it's time to bring out your lens of introspection. This is where you ask the hard questions. Can you see yourself filling this gap? Does addressing this need resonate with your passions and values? Can your strengths provide a solution that's not just effective, but unique?

Week 1: Choosing the right platforms for your brand

Not all platforms will align with your brand's goals or your audience's preferences. This week involves researching where your target audience spends their time and determining which platforms offer the best opportunity to connect with them.

Week 2: Creating a personal branding website

Your personal branding website act as the central hub for your online presence. Laying the foundation for a website that effectively communicates your brand's message, showcases your portfolio or services, will offer valuable content to your audience. Focus on essential elements such as a clear homepage, an about section that tells your story, a blog, or resources section for your content, and contact information.

Week 3: Social media strategy for personal branding

With your website set up, work on developing a comprehensive social media strategy. This strategy should align with your overall branding goals, aiming to grow your following, engage with your audience, and reinforce your brand message across selected platforms.

Week 4: Blogging, podcasting, and video

Whether you're writing blog posts, recording podcasts, or producing videos, your content should provide value to your audience while highlighting your expertise and personality.

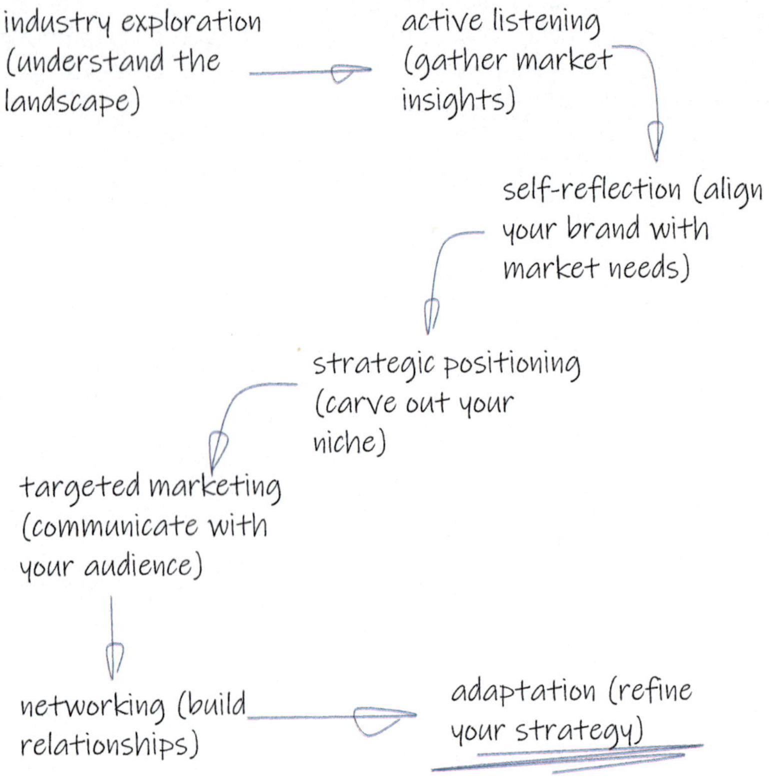
industry exploration (understand the landscape)
active listening (gather market insights)
self-reflection (align your brand with market needs)
strategic positioning (carve out your niche)
targeted marketing (communicate with your audience)
networking (build relationships)
adaptation (refine your strategy)

MONTH 3

Must-read: **"Building a storybrand: clarify your message so customers will listen"** by Donald Miller

Focus: clarify and strengthen your brand's story and messaging.

BRAND MESSAGE

Now it's a good time to showcase your business's brand identity and to create a unique place among the many competitors. This time is focused on improving your brand's message and ensuring it communicates clearly and coherently through every channel of interaction.

The secret of a strong brand rests in its visual aesthetic, its ability to build recognition and cultivate loyalty among consumers. A brand that communicates its values and proposition with clarity not only stands out but also builds a deeper connection with its audience.

1 - The message
Inspect your brand's language, imagery, and emotions it transmits. Is your message clear? Does it resonate? Is it memorable?

2 - The visuals
Every touchpoint, from your website to your packaging, from your social media profiles to your customer service scripts, should have the same tonality. Consistency breeds familiarity, and familiarity breeds' trust. You're ensuring that your brand looks, feels, and speaks in harmony.

GOOD TO KNOW
Storytelling isn't just for books. It's an effective tool in your marketing collection. Your brand's story - its origins, its journey, its values can establish a powerful connection with your audience.

CTA: Examine your brand's guidelines. Is your brand up to date? Does it reflect your true brand identity?

SUSTAINABLE MARKETING: DIGITAL ENGAGEMENT

As the calendar turns to Month 3, the focus for sustainable marketing pivots towards leveraging the digital world. This month's emphasis on digital engagement recognises the powerful role that digital platforms play in your strategy. Keep reviewing and updating your message regularly to ensure that it matches your sustainability goals and adapts to new policies and guidelines. Be aware of the newest digital trends and technologies that can improve your sustainable marketing efforts.

1 - Strategies for effective digital engagement
Maximise social media impact: Utilise social media platforms to promote sustainable practices and share eco-friendly content.

Content marketing for sustainability: Blogs, videos, infographics, and podcasts can be powerful tools to educate and engage your audience on environmental issues.

Enhance website: Optimise your website for energy efficiency. This includes using eco-friendly web hosting, optimising images, and videos for faster loading times, and ensuring mobile-friendly design.

Leverage eco-friendly authorities: Collaborate with experts who are advocates for sustainability. Their endorsement can help amplify your brand's sustainable message to a broader audience.

To-do: Develop strategies for effective digital engagement.

GENERATIVE AI CHEAT SHEET: PLANNING AHEAD

Month 3 is about looking forward. It's a critical time for evaluating and reviewing performance, using tools and software to revise strategies. Examples from different industries highlight the impact of well-used reports. These stories show how organisations have changed possible challenges into chances for growth by adapting their strategies based on quarterly results.

Prompt 1: "Analyse the importance of quarterly reviews in steering company objectives."
Application: Provide content that is based on data analysis and quantifiable outcomes and evaluate how well it works to modify strategies.

Prompt 2: "Discuss how to effectively use quarterly reports to inform future decisions."
Application: Share tips or success stories on leveraging quarterly reports for strategic planning and operational improvements.

PERSONAL BRAND: PRESENCE

The digital landscape is as vast as it is diverse; understanding social media is both an advantage and a necessity. Consistency is your anchor. Your social media presence should be a seamless extension of your personal brand narrative, echoing your core message, values, and visual identity across all platforms.

Week 1: Planning your personal branding content
The month begins with the creation of a content calendar - a strategic tool for planning, organising, and scheduling your content across various platforms. This first week focus on identifying key themes, topics, and formats that align with your brand's goals and resonate with your target audience.

Week 2: Storytelling techniques to improve your brand
Storytelling is a powerful way to humanise your brand, build emotional connections, and differentiate yourself in a crowded digital landscape. During the second week, focus on refining your storytelling skills. Explore different narrative techniques that can make your content more compelling.

Week 3: SEO basics for personal branding
Understanding the basics of Search Engine Optimisation (SEO) is essential for ensuring that your content reaches your intended audience. Learning how to optimise your content for search engines, covering key topics such as keyword research, on-page SEO (like using the right tags and structuring your content effectively), and off- page SEO tactics, will help your brand have the visibility it deserves.

Week 4: Engaging your audience
Engage with your audience by creating content that invites and responds to feedback, and by facilitating conversations that help them bond with you and each other. You can host live Q&A sessions, launch campaigns that involve user-generated content, or provide special content to your most loyal followers.

the hook

- primary needs
- opening statement
- relatable language

the message

- key benefits
- differentiator
- achievements
- expertise

the takeaway

- outcomes
- "why"
- compelling
- memorable

Integrate the hook, the core message, and the takeaway into a seamless, cohesive personal brand statement.

MONTH 4

Must-read: **"Hooked: how to build habit-forming products"** by Nir Eyal

Focus: how to make your products indispensable and habit- forming.

CONTENT STRATEGY

At the heart of every thriving business sits a compelling content marketing strategy, a foundation that not only draws audiences in but builds lasting connections based on trust and shared value. Your content should reach an audience and connect with them, turning your brand into a reference.

Content marketing exceeds communication; it's an expression of your brand's narrative, shaped to meet your audience's needs and challenges. This month, think about the endless possibilities that lie in reimagining our approach to content.

1 - Data-driven content

Intuition is invaluable, but data is definitive. Look at content views, shares, comments, and time spent on page to identify patterns and preferences. Use this data to tailor your content calendar, focusing on subjects that have proven to engage your audience.

2 - Segmentation

Beyond general analytics, segmentation allows for a more nuanced approach to content creation. By categorising your audience based on demographics, behaviour, or purchase history, you can create more personalised and relevant content that speaks directly to the specific needs and interests of different segments.

GOOD TO KNOW

Content marketing is not a static field; it evolves with every shift in consumer behaviour and technological advancement. Keeping abreast of these changes, understanding the latest trends in content consumption, and adopting innovative content formats can significantly enhance your strategy's effectiveness and your brand's relevance.

CTA: determine what truly captivates your audience. Use these insights to fine-tune your content calendar, spotlighting topics that spark interest and interaction.

Utilise the power of both digital platforms and the irreplaceable value of face-to-face interactions to amplify your message across your audience.

SUSTAINABLE MARKETING: PRODUCTION AND PACKAGING

Focusing on sustainable production and packaging allows businesses to solidify their position as environmentally responsible entities. Start by auditing your production and packaging processes and identify areas for sustainable improvement. Then, take these green strides to your audience. Educate them, engage them, and inspire them through your sustainable journey. Use your platforms to tell the story of how your products are made, the eco-friendly materials you use, and the steps you're taking to minimise environmental impact.

1 - Advocating for sustainable production
Be open about your manufacturing processes. Share how your products are made, emphasising the sustainable practices employed.

Eco-friendly materials: Highlight the use of sustainable materials in your products. Whether it's organic fabrics, recycled plastics, informing customers about these choices helps the decision-making process.

Minimalistic packaging design: Adopt a minimalistic approach to packaging. Reducing unnecessary packaging not only lessens waste but also resonates with consumers who prefer simplicity and eco- conscious choices.

Reducing production waste: Share initiatives aimed at reducing waste during production, showcasing these efforts can enhance your brand's environmental credibility.

To-do: Audit your production and packaging and make sustainability a core part of your brand story.

GENERATIVE AI CHEAT SHEET: RELATIONSHIP BUILDING

Emphasise the importance of building and nurturing business relationships through industry events, and partnership opportunities. The value of face-to-face interactions and the strategic alliances formed through these interactions cannot be overstated.

Prompt 1: "Illustrate the benefits of networking events for B2B organisations."
Application: Promote corporate retreats and industry events, focusing on the value of in-person interactions and partnership formations.

Prompt 2: "Discuss strategies for building long-term business partnerships."
Application: Provide guidance on nurturing relationships, highlighting success stories from summer networking events.

Refine your prompting skills.
Try meta-prompts: meta-prompts are when you ask ChatGPT to explain how it would do a task, instead of doing the task itself. This can be a good way to create new ideas or plans.

PERSONAL BRAND: NETWORKING

Your personal brand can benefit from connecting and partnering with others. By interacting with industry colleagues, working with compatible brands, and offering your knowledge through different channels, you will boost your brand's exposure and trustworthiness.

Week 1: Networking strategies for personal branding
Developing effective networking strategies that align with your personal brand goals involves identifying key industry events, both online and offline, where you can connect with peers and thought leaders.

Week 2: Collaborating with other brands and influencers
Collaboration is a powerful tool for expanding your brand's reach. Collaboration can take many forms, from co-creating content to cross-promotion on social media.

Week 3: Guest blogging and podcast appearances
Guest blogging and podcast appearances are excellent ways to share your expertise with a broader audience.

Week 4: Hosting webinars and workshops
Hosting webinars and workshops is a direct way to engage with your audience, showcase your expertise, and provide value.

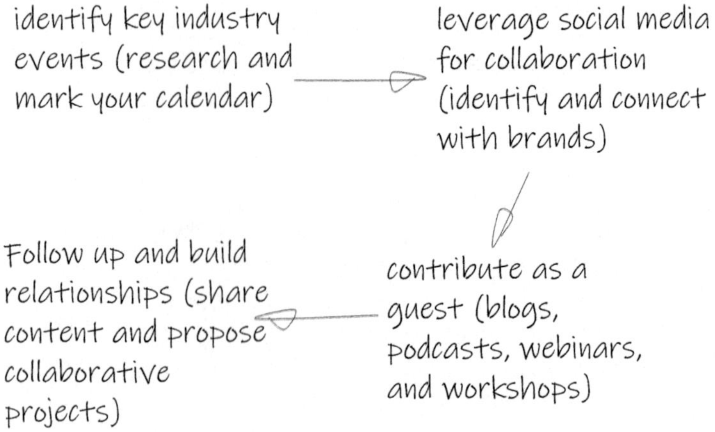
identify key industry events (research and mark your calendar)
leverage social media for collaboration (identify and connect with brands)
contribute as a guest (blogs, podcasts, webinars, and workshops)
Follow up and build relationships (share content and propose collaborative projects)

MONTH 5

Must-read: **"This is Marketing: you can't be seen until you learn to see"** by Seth Godin

Focus: revisit your marketing strategies and philosophies with insights from one of the greats.

DIGITAL AND SEO

Your approach to SEO and online marketing should be both meticulous and fluid, adapting to changing algorithms of search engines and the behaviours of our audience. It's a commitment to not only remain visible but to resonate on a level that goes beyond the superficial.

Preparing your website and content for search engines is like getting ready for a big show, making sure that when our audience comes, they'll join a conversation that educates and inspires.

The ongoing journey of SEO requires you to be both explorer and learner, constantly researching and updating your strategies to align with the latest trends and best practices.

1 - Online presence

Your commitment to continuous improvement, strategic optimisation, and deep understanding of our audience's needs will light your path towards achieving unparalleled visibility and engagement.

2 - Tools

Begin with comprehensive SEO audit tools like SEMrush, Ahrefs, or Moz. These platforms offer deep insights into your website's current SEO performance, highlighting areas for improvement such as broken links, page speed issues, and keyword optimisation opportunities.

GOOD TO KNOW

When working on optimisation, prioritise long-tail keywords. These specific, often less competitive phrases offer a clearer path to better targeting and higher conversion rates. You can create content that matches the precise interests and search terms of your audience by concentrating on long-tail keywords, making your digital presence more fitting and effective.

Begin with a comprehensive SEO audit of your website, assess the current state of your online presence identifying strengths to build upon and weakness to address.

SUSTAINABLE MARKETING: ENGAGEMENT AND ADVOCACY

It's time to recognise and leverage the power of your team in driving forward your sustainability agenda. Encourage, empower, and engage them to become active participants and advocates in your sustainable marketing efforts. When your team believes in your mission, they can become your most influential ambassadors. Adopt a culture where sustainability is both a corporate goal and a shared mission.

1 - Cultivating a culture of sustainability
Organise educational sessions and workshops – the definition, the importance, and the way the business is implementing it.

Encouraging sustainable practices in the workplace such as recycling programs, reducing energy consumption, or encouraging public transport or cycling to work.

Fosus on employee-led sustainability initiatives. Create platforms for employees to propose and lead sustainability initiatives.

Involve colleagues in campaigns. Feature employees in marketing campaigns related to sustainability.

Equip colleagues to be brand advocates. Provide employees with information and tools to talk about the company's sustainability initiatives.

To-do: Encourage, empower, and engage employees and colleagues in your sustainable marketing efforts.

GENERATIVE AI CHEAT SHEET: FORECASTING

Now, the focus is on strategic forecasting and planning, essential components for equipping businesses with the foresight and strategies necessary to prepare for the future effectively. The use of forecasting tools is central to this process, providing businesses with data-driven insights and predictions about market trends, customer behaviour, and potential challenges.

Prompt 1: “Explain the role of strategic forecasting in Q2 preparation."
Application: Create content around the use of forecasting tools and how they contribute to effective Q2 strategies.

Prompt 2: "Highlight the benefits of attending strategic planning workshops."
Application: Promote workshops, emphasising their role in helping businesses stay ahead and adapt to market changes.

PERSONAL BRAND: VISUALS

This month, we will explore how personal branding can benefit from visual elements that make your brand stand out and stick in people's minds. Improving your visual branding means creating a consistent and attractive image that connects with your audience and sets you apart from competitors.

develop a brand style guide (detail your brand's colour palette, typography, logo, etc)

invest in professional photography (schedule a photoshoot that aligns with your brand's image)

optimise visual consistency (ensure visual elements are consistent across platforms)

incorporate visual branding (use brand colours for graphics and maintain a consistent style)

engage in visual storytelling (include infographics, branded quotes, behind-the-scenes photos, or storytelling through video)

Week 1: Designing your brand
Design or revisit important elements of your brand to ensure they accurately reflect your brand's personality and appeal to your target audience.

Week 2: Photoshoot tips for personal branding
High-quality photos are essential for personal branding, providing a human touch and building trust with your audience. Plan and execute a photoshoot that captures your brand's essence.

Week 3: Creating consistent visuals across all platforms.
Ensure that your colour schemes, fonts, and imagery are consistent across your website, social media, and any other marketing materials.

Week 4: Video branding essentials
Incorporating your visual branding into your video content. This includes using your brand's colour scheme in graphics, displaying your logo at key points, and maintaining a consistent style and tone throughout your videos.

MONTH 6

Must-read: **"The culture code: the secrets of highly successful groups"** by Daniel Coyle

Focus: team dynamics and building a successful marketing team culture.

MID-YEAR REVIEW

You have reached the midpoint of your marketing journey. It's a good time to pause, reflect, and recalibrate. The mid-year review is an important moment in the marketing calendar, it's a time to review your strategies, measure their performance, and make the necessary adjustments.

Analise the data and feedback collected over the past months to understand what has worked, what hasn't, and why. This exercise in data analysis is also a strategic opportunity to enhance your marketing approach, ensuring that it is robust, resilient, and responsive to the ever-evolving market landscape.

1 - Agile marketing
Marketing agility is about building a culture and system that supports ongoing learning and fast reaction to new data. Using more adaptable tools and processes can improve your team's ability to respond to shifts in the market or strategy. Use an iterative approach for your campaigns. Rather than ending a campaign, adjust based on real-time data.

2 - Strategic pivots
Once you've identified the need for a pivot, plan your execution carefully. Define clear objectives for the pivot, set measurable goals, and communicate changes effectively within your team. Ensure that all stakeholders understand the rationale behind the pivot and their role in implementing it.

GOOD TO KNOW
Agile marketing strategies allow you to quickly and easily adjust to new information, developments, and possibilities, making sure that your marketing actions stay current and efficient.

Incorporating flexibility and adaptability into your marketing strategies is both beneficial and essential. These qualities allow you to swiftly react to new insights, trends, and opportunities, thereby ensuring that your marketing efforts are consistently relevant and impactful.

SUSTAINABLE MARKETING: CUSTOMER AWARENESS

This month, be proactive in informing your customers or clients, transforming them into informed actors in the sustainability movement. Use captivating content, compelling stories, and dynamic platforms to convey the significance of sustainability in your industry.

1 - Strategies for effective customer education
Develop a content marketing strategy centred around sustainability. This could include blog posts, videos, infographics, and social media content that inform customers about environmental issues and how your products or services provide sustainable solutions.

Use storytelling to show the importance of sustainability. Tell stories about where your products come from, how they are made with sustainable practices, or how your services help protect the environment.

Partner with environmental experts, NGOs, or influencers who can lend credibility to your educational content and help expand its reach.

Be transparent about your company's sustainability practices and progress. Honest communication builds trust and reinforces the educational aspect of your marketing.

To-do: Inspire an audience that chooses sustainability as a way of life.

GENERATIVE AI CHEAT SHEET: GAINING MOMENTUM

Adopting agile marketing strategies and understanding when and how to strategically pivot can significantly impact business success.

Prompt 1: "Provide a detailed guide on how to craft agile marketing strategies that accommodate rapid changes in the marketing environment. Discuss the principles of agile marketing, including continuous improvement and flexibility, and how these principles can be applied to marketing campaign development."

Application: Develop a template for an agile marketing plan that outlines how marketing teams can apply agile principles to their campaign strategies.

Prompt 2: "Explain the process of identifying when a strategic pivot is necessary in marketing and the steps to successfully implement these changes. Discuss how to use market feedback, performance data, and competitive analysis to make informed decisions about pivoting."

Application: Organise a series of workshops for marketing leaders on how to execute strategic pivots effectively.

Refine your prompting skills.
Break down your questions: if you want to ask about something complex, make a sequence of questions that follow from one another in a logical way. This can help ChatGPT give more consistent and complete answers.

PERSONAL BRAND: SOCIAL MEDIA

This month focus on social media strategies, capitalising on the unique strengths of each platform to enhance your personal brand. Refine your presence on key social networks, with tailored strategies to grow your audience, and engage effectively. Learn the nuances of Instagram, LinkedIn, YouTube, etc and use these platforms to showcase your expertise, connect with your audience, and amplify your brand's reach.

optimise social media (optimised profiles form the foundation of our social media strategy)

diversify your content strategy (tailor your content to each platform's unique strengths)

actively engage with your audience (respond to comments and participate in discussions)

utilise hashtags and trends strategically (research and use relevant hashtags and participate in trending topics)

host live sessions and webinars (enhance real-time engagement with your audience, showcase your expertise)

Week 1: Strategies for growth
This week, explore strategies to enhance your social media presence, including optimising your profile, using high-quality images and videos, engaging with Instagram stories and reels, and employing hashtags effectively.

Week 2: Leveraging LinkedIn for professional branding
LinkedIn stands as the premier professional networking platform, essential for establishing your professional brand. Share insightful articles, participate in discussions, and connect with industry leaders to enhance your visibility and authority in your field. LinkedIn is an invaluable tool for networking, generating leads, and showcasing your professional achievements.

Week 3: Branding tactics
Develop a content strategy that provides value to your audience, whether through educational content, entertainment, or insights into your industry.

Week 4: Engagement
Different platforms offer unique opportunities for real-time interaction, sharing news, and participating in broader conversations within your industry. Focus on concise, engaging content, timely interactions, and the strategic use of hashtags. Utilise each platform's groups, live videos, and targeted posts to create a unique community and drive discussions.

Insight:
Employ platform-specific strategies that effectively grow your audience, engage in meaningful interactions, and showcase unique facets of your personal brand.

MONTH 7

Must-read: **"Killing Marketing: How innovative businesses are turning marketing cost into profit"** by Joe Pulizzi and Robert Rose

Focus: learn how to revamp traditional marketing strategies for better ROI.

RETENTION

Your goal for the year is to strengthen the relationships with your clients. In month 7, work on maintaining those ties, turning occasional prospects into faithful supporters through planned outreach and loyalty programs.

Using customised marketing strategies and improving the customer experience, will make your clients feel valued and acknowledged - not just as sales, but as important parts of your brand's community.

The goal is to create a customer experience so compelling that it not only encourages repeat business but also promotes genuine brand loyalty. This effort requires a careful combination of data-driven insights and a heartfelt commitment to treating customers as valued partners in your brand's journey.

1 - Personalisation

Utilise data analytics to understand costumer behaviours, preferences, and purchase history. This information becomes the foundation for creating personalised messages and offers that resonate on an individual level. Invest in technology platforms that enable dynamic content creation and delivery. Tools like AI and machine learning can help predict customer preferences and automate personalised communication, ensuring that each customer feels uniquely valued.

2 - Loyalty programmes

Develop loyalty programmes that go beyond transactional rewards. Consider incorporating elements of gamification, exclusive experiences, or community building to deepen the customer's emotional connection to the brand.

GOOD TO KNOW

Keeping existing clients is more cost effective than finding new ones, to what concerns to customer relationships. This benefit is not only about saving money; it also creates a solid base of loyalty that helps to increase the revenue over time and, importantly, promote the brand.

Utilise personalisation and innovative loyalty programs to transform casual buyers into loyal brand advocates. Data analytics will help you gain deep insights into customer behaviours, preferences, and purchase histories.

SUSTAINABLE MARKETING: ENERGY EFFICIENCY

Commit to implementing energy-saving practices within your organisation and use your influence to promote the importance of energy efficiency. Educate, engage, and empower both your employees, colleagues, and consumers to make more energy-efficient choices. Businesses should not only implement energy-saving practices within their operations but also use their marketing platforms to advocate for and educate about energy efficiency. The goal is to highlight the importance of reducing energy consumption, both as a means of protecting the environment and reducing costs, and to position the business as a leader in sustainable practices.

1 - Promoting energy efficiency in business operations:
Begin by conducting an energy audit to identify areas where energy consumption can be reduced. This could include upgrading to energy-efficient lighting, optimising heating and encouraging energy- saving habits among employees.

Implementing energy-efficient solutions: Invest in energy-efficient technologies and implement policies that promote energy efficiency.

Educational campaigns: Use your marketing platforms to educate consumers about the importance of energy efficiency. This can include tips on reducing energy consumption, the benefits of energy- efficient appliances, or the cost savings associated with reduced energy use.

To-do: Implement energy efficient operations.

GENERATIVE AI CHEAT SHEET: YEAR-END SUCCESS

As businesses venture further into the year, the focus naturally shifts towards nurturing connections, transforming casual buyers into loyal brand advocates. This key phase of strategic engagement and retention efforts aims not only to enhance the customer experience but also to adopt a sense of belonging and appreciation among the customer base.

Prompt 1: "Explore strategies for enhancing the customer experience through personalisation. Discuss how data analytics can be utilised to understand customer behaviours".
Application: Create a comprehensive toolkit for marketers that outlines practical steps for implementing personalisation strategies in their campaigns.

Prompt 2: "Discuss the importance of loyalty programs in building brand loyalty and deepening customer connections. Highlight innovative approaches to loyalty programs, such as incorporating gamification, offering exclusive experiences, and fostering community engagement."
Application: Organise a workshop for business owners and marketers focused on designing innovative loyalty programs.

Refine your prompting skills.
Invoke role-play: ask ChatGPT to assume a specific role, such as a teacher explaining a concept to a student or a consultant advising a business. This can tailor the tone and approach of the response.

PERSONAL BRAND: MAINTENANCE

This chapter of your branding journey highlights the importance of maintenance and growth, ensuring that the brand you present to the world remains relevant, and true to your evolving professional narrative. Reflect on your brand's journey, assess its current standing, and make strategic adjustments to align with your future aspirations. This month, innovation, brand maintenance, alongside proven tactics, and methodologies, plays a crucial role in reinforcing your brand's integrity and appeal.

implement online monitoring (utilise advanced social listening tools to monitor your brand's online presence actively)

develop a response strategy (create a guideline for responding to negative feedback that emphasises empathy)

refresh your brand to stay relevant (conduct a thorough brand audit to assess your current branding elements)

use testimonials and reviews for brand credibility (actively seek testimonials and reviews and feature these testimonials prominently on your website)

Week 1: Monitoring your online reputation
Using new methods and technologies to monitor how people talk about your brand on different platforms is important. This way, you can be prepared for the story, acknowledging positive interactions, and responding to any misunderstandings or difficulties quickly.

Week 2: Handling negative feedback and criticism
No brand is immune to criticism, but the way you respond can significantly impact your brand's resilience and perception. Focus on strategies for managing negative feedback with grace and professionalism.

Week 3: Updating your brand
As your professional journey evolves, so too should your brand. The third week is dedicated to the thoughtful consideration of your brand's current image and the strategic updates required to keep it fresh and aligned with your goals. This could involve refreshing your brand visuals, revising your messaging to reflect new directions or achievements, or even redefining your target audience.

Week 4: The power of testimonials and reviews
Encouraging satisfied clients, customers, or followers to share their experiences not only enhances your brand's credibility but also provides valuable social proof that can attract new opportunities and reinforce your brand's positive reputation.

This month's emphasis on maintenance, adaptation, and engagement with both your audience and the feedback they provide sets the stage for sustained brand growth.

MONTH 8

Must-read: **"Made to stick: Why some ideas survive, and others die"** by Chip Heath and Dan Heath

Focus: understand what makes ideas memorable and impactful.

SOCIAL MEDIA AND INFLUENCER MARKETING

This month, concentrate on using social media and influencers effectively to boost your brand's awareness and reputation. Social media and influencer marketing are powerful ways to enhance a brand's voice and spread its message. Producing content that connects and motivates sharing, transforms your audience into brand supporters. Collaborating with influencers who reflect your brand values strengthens this impact, reaching new audiences and building confidence in your brand.

Each social media platform has its unique strengths and audience behaviours. Tailor your content and influencer collaborations to fit the specific dynamics of each platform. For example, visually driven stories on Instagram, thought leadership articles on LinkedIn, or engaging video content on TikTok. Understanding these nuances enhances the effectiveness of your social media strategy.

1 - Approach

Social media is a diverse and changing landscape, so you need to be flexible and intentional in your strategy. Social media platforms give you a direct connection to your audience, letting you interact and receive feedback in real time. Produce content that matches both your brand's voice and the current trends and conversations that interest your audience. This relevance is what turns passive watchers into engaged supporters of your brand's story.

2 – Measuring success

Use data and analytics to measure the impact of your social media and influencer marketing activities. How well your audience engages, converts, and grows are important signs of how well your content and partnerships are connecting with your ideal customers. Use these insights to constantly improve your approach, making sure that your social media and influencer marketing strategies stay flexible and adaptive to the changing digital environment.

GOOD TO KNOW

The return on investment (ROI) from influencer marketing can significantly exceed traditional marketing methods, provided there's a strong alignment between the influencer's audience and your target demographic. The authenticity and trust that influencers have cultivated with their followers translate into higher engagement and conversion rates for the brands they endorse.

Determine the most relevant metrics for your social media and influencer marketing campaigns, focusing on engagement rates, conversion metrics (such as click-through rates and sales conversions), and audience growth.

SUSTAINABLE MARKETING: ETHICAL CONSUMERISM

Ethical consumerism is the idea of choosing products and services that follow ethical standards, such as fair employment, environmental protection, and animal rights. It's a consumer behaviour based on ethical principles and an awareness of the consequences of one's buying choices. Businesses can use their marketing tactics to promote and facilitate it. The emphasis is on showing the value of making buying decisions that are not only good for the individual but also helpful for society and the environment.

1-Promoting ethical consumerism in marketing
Use your marketing platforms to educate consumers about how their purchasing decisions can impact the environment, society, and the economy.

Highlighting ethically sourced products
Specifically highlight products or services that are ethically sourced and produced. This could include items made with fair trade practices, eco-friendly materials, or from sustainable sources.

Collaborating with ethical brands
Partner with other ethical brands to create collaborative campaigns.

Customer feedback: Gather feedback from customers about their perceptions and attitudes towards ethical consumerism.

To-do: Create an information campaign on ethical consumerism.

GENERATIVE AI CHEAT SHEET: MARKET TRENDS

Social media and influencer marketing stand out as important elements in shaping a brand's visibility and credibility. With the vast array of platforms available, each offering unique opportunities to connect with audiences, it's a requirement for brands to strategically leverage these tools to amplify their voice and extend their reach.

Prompt 1: Draft a guide on creating dynamic and deliberate social media content strategies that align with brand voice and audience interests across different platforms."
Application: Develop a comprehensive social media content calendar tool that helps marketers plan and execute a dynamic content strategy.

Prompt 2: " Explain how to implement metrics and analytics for measuring the success of social media and influencer marketing campaigns."
Application: Create an analytics dashboard that integrates with various social media platforms and influencer marketing tools to provide real-time insights into campaign performance.

Refine your prompting skills.
Start your prompt with a concise context or background information and specify the domain or topic you want to discuss, then break it down (write a function that calculates [task]).

PERSONAL BRAND: ADVANCED CONTENT

This month is about exploring more than just creating and sharing content, but also looking at the details of advanced techniques that can greatly boost your brand's exposure and interaction. By using a smart combination of SEO, email marketing, lead generation, and paid advertising, you're on the way to raise your personal brand into a higher level of influence and authority.

Week 1: Advanced SEO strategies for personal brands
Kicking off the month, the focus shifts to working on advanced SEO strategies tailored to the unique needs and goals of personal brands. This involves moving beyond basic keyword optimisation to explore sophisticated techniques such as voice search optimisation, local SEO for personal branding, and the strategic use of long-tail keywords in your content.

Week 2: Email marketing for personal branding
Consider email marketing, a great tool for personal branding that, when executed correctly, increases connections with your audience. Personalised email campaigns speak directly to the interests and needs of your subscribers. From segmenting your email list to automating personalised email sequences, the goal is to engage your audience with valuable content that reinforces your brand's value proposition and builds lasting relationships.

Week 3: Creating lead magnets and freebies
The focus shifts to the production of captivating lead magnets and freebies - a tactic that aims to draw and maintain the attention of possible followers and customers. This requires creating high-quality resources such as e-books, webinars, templates, or courses that your audience can get by giving their contact information. The main point is to provide something of real worth that not only demonstrates your skills but also leads to more interaction with your brand.

Week 4: Paid advertising, should you invest?
From understanding the nuances of platform-specific advertising (such as Google Ads, Facebook Ads, and LinkedIn Sponsored Content) to creating targeted ad campaigns that resonate with your audience, the focus is on making informed decisions that align with your branding goals and budget constraints.

Work on advanced SEO techniques, personalised email marketing, valuable lead magnets, and strategic paid advertising to spread your message – ensuring it lands with impact, engage authentically, and contributes to sustained growth.

MONTH 9

Must read: **"The 1-page marketing plan: get new customers, make more money, and stand out from the crowd"** by Allan Dib

Focus: simplify your marketing strategies, set a clear path for the coming year.

SEASONAL MARKETING

Month 9 is the time to get things done. It's when we use all our insights, ideas, and efforts and focus them on getting ready for our main marketing campaigns – time critical sales, end-of-year promotions, etc. Set clear goals, plan each activity, and make sure you have everything you need to complete them. By starting early, you will have an advantage, and you can make changes without stress. Getting ready for the Big Push is essential, which means being careful with your strategy and adaptable in our execution.

1 – Checklist review
Before any campaign goes live, run through a comprehensive pre-launch checklist. This should cover everything from content accuracy and channel readiness to technical checks like website load times and mobile responsiveness. Confirm that tracking codes are properly installed for analytics and that all team members are briefed on their roles post-launch.

2 – Real-time monitoring
Once your campaign is live, don't just set it and forget it. Schedule daily (or even hourly, for high-stakes campaigns) monitoring sessions. Use these sessions to review performance data, social media engagement, and customer feedback in real-time. This proactive approach allows you to quickly identify and address any issues, adjust strategies to improve performance, and capitalize on unexpected opportunities to enhance campaign effectiveness.

GOOD TO KNOW
Understanding the importance of timing in the execution of marketing campaigns is essential for any marketer looking to maximise their impact. Incorporating this level of strategic timing into your campaign planning involves rigorous analysis and forecasting. It may also require testing different launch times for smaller initiatives to gather data on what works best for your specific audience.

SUSTAINABLE MARKETING: REVIEW

Month 9 offers an opportunity to examine where the business stands on its sustainability journey and to chart a course for the future. During this period, you should assess the impact of the strategies employed, celebrate successes, learn from challenges, and plan for the forthcoming year's sustainable endeavours. Conducting a year-end review is a retrospective exercise and a strategic stepping stone for future planning. It involves evaluating the effectiveness of sustainable marketing initiatives, understanding their impact on both the business and the environment, and gathering insights that will shape future strategies.

1- Publishing a sustainability report

Compile a comprehensive report detailing the sustainable initiatives undertaken throughout the year. This should include both the successes and the challenges encountered, providing an honest overview of the company's sustainability journey.

Measuring impact: Utilise data and metrics to quantify the impact of your sustainable marketing strategies. This can include metrics like reductions in carbon footprint, waste reduction, increases in sustainable product sales, or engagement levels in sustainability- focused campaigns.

Incorporating stakeholder feedback: Engage with stakeholders, including customers, employees, and partners, to gather feedback and ideas for future sustainable initiatives. This collaborative approach can lead to more innovative and inclusive strategies.

Setting new goals: Based on the insights gained from the year-end review, set goals for the upcoming year. These should be both ambitious and achievable, pushing the business towards greater sustainability.

Let the actionable insights from your review guide your strategies, enabling your business to thrive sustainably in the years to come.

GENERATIVE AI CHEAT SHEET: ACHIEVEMENTS

Month 9 is a time to summarise the year's achievements and show gratitude to clients and partners through year-end reviews, and appreciation events.

Prompt 1: "Discuss the importance of year-end reviews in celebrating successes and setting future goals."
Application: Offer guidelines on conducting meaningful year-end reviews and using them to strategize for the coming year.

Prompt 2: "Share creative ways to show client appreciation during the holiday season."
Application: Provide ideas for thoughtful client gifts and memorable appreciation events.

Refine your prompting skills.
Leverage recent contexts: if your task builds on recent information or a previous interaction, summarize that context in your prompt. This helps ChatGPT provide more relevant and connected responses.

PERSONAL BRAND: GROWTH

The ninth chapter of your personal branding journey pivots towards the core of your brand's essence: your own personal development. This month emphasises the undeniable link between self-growth and brand enhancement. It's a period dedicated to broadening your horizons, refining your skills, and achieving a balance that reflects positively on your personal brand.

Week 1: Continuous learning and skill enhancement
The month begins with a commitment to lifelong learning and skill enhancement. This week, identify areas for growth and pursue opportunities to enhance your expertise, whether through formal education, online courses, workshops, or self-study. The goal is to ensure that your personal brand remains relevant and authoritative, grounded in a foundation of ever-expanding knowledge and capabilities.

Week 2: Public speaking and presentation skills
The ability to communicate effectively and captivate an audience is invaluable for any personal brand. This includes practicing techniques to improve your delivery, storytelling, and audience engagement, whether in face-to-face settings or through digital platforms.

Week 3: Writing and publishing a book for brand authority
This week explore the process of turning your expertise and unique insights into a published work that can serve as a tangible manifestation of your personal brand. Whether it's a how-to guide, or a thought leadership piece, authoring a book is a powerful way to share your knowledge, tell your story, and solidify your status as an expert in your field.

Week 4: Work-life balance and personal branding
The emphasis turns to the importance of maintaining a healthy work- life balance. A strong personal brand is supported by a well-rounded, fulfilled individual. Find the balance between professional pursuits and personal well-being, ensuring that your brand's growth does not come at the expense of your health, or happiness.

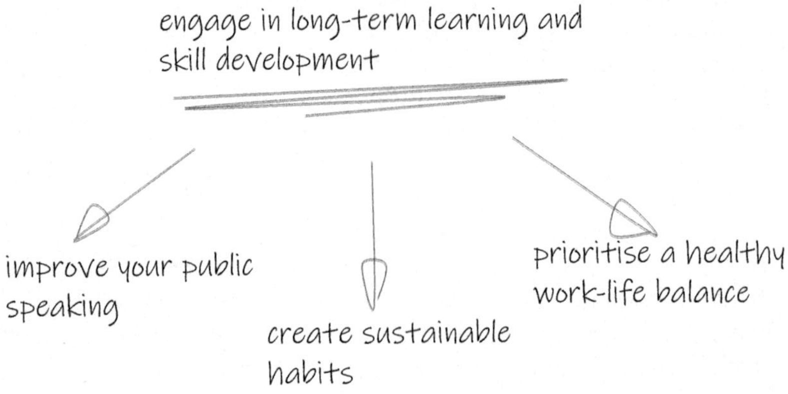

Committing to continuous learning, refining key communication skills, sharing your expertise through authorship, a maintaining a balanced life, you strengthen the foundation of your personal brand.

MONTH 10

Must read: **"Atomic Habits"** by James Clear

Focus: building productive habits and routines that will enhance your marketing strategies and personal efficiency.

MAJOR CAMPAIGNS

The main goal of Month 10 is to launch and manage your major marketing initiatives smoothly. As these campaigns progress, your focus is to make sure they are done perfectly, reaching, and engaging your audience well. This needs a proactive approach to track performance metrics as they happen and the ability to adjust strategies quickly, improving your campaigns' effectiveness and increasing their influence.

Set up a real-time monitoring dashboard. This dashboard should aggregate data from all active campaign channels, providing instant access to key performance indicators (KPIs) such as website traffic, engagement rates, conversion metrics, and social media interactions. Having this information at your fingertips allows for immediate insights into how the campaign is performing across different platforms and audiences. It enables you to identify trends, pinpoint issues, and uncover opportunities for optimisation as the campaign progresses.

1 – Engagement patterns
Understanding and leveraging the specific times when your audience is most engaged can significantly amplify your campaign's impact. Dive into analytics to find patterns in user engagement across different times of the day or days of the week. Use this data to schedule your most critical campaign elements.

2 – Mirco-segmentation
Going beyond basic demographic segmentation to embrace micro-segmentation allows you to tailor your messaging and offers to very specific audience groups, based on their behaviours, preferences, and past interactions with your brand. Use data analytics tools to break down your audience into smaller, more defined segments based on detailed criteria such as purchase history, browsing behaviour, and engagement levels.

GOOD TO KNOW
By continuously monitoring your campaign's performance and being prepared to make swift adjustments, you can enhance its effectiveness in real-time. This might involve reallocating budget to high-performing channels, tweaking messaging to better resonate with your audience, or adjusting targeting criteria to reach a more relevant segment.

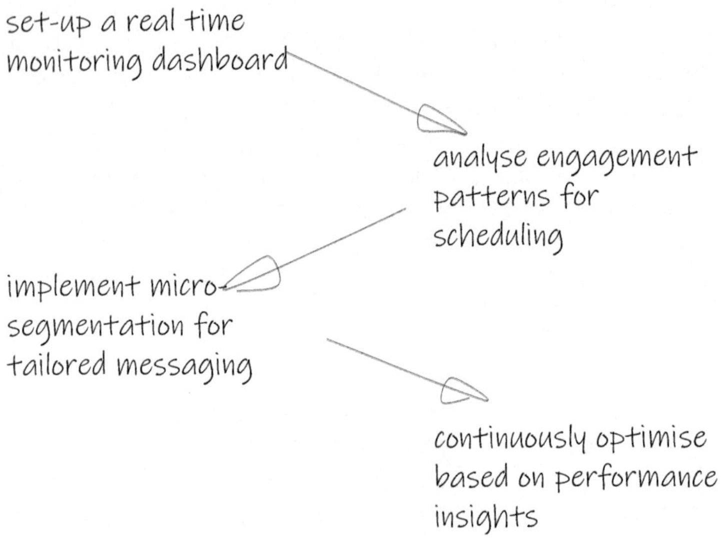

CTA: Focus on real-time monitoring and embrace the principles of agile optimisation to meet and exceed your campaign goals.

SUSTAINABLE MARKETING: NEW INITIATIVES AND RESOLUTIONS

This month, set a precedent for the months to come. Whether it's through educational campaigns, interactive sustainability challenges, or incentivising eco-friendly customer behaviour, every action you take now lays the groundwork for a greener future. Begin by introducing innovative eco-friendly products or services and implement meaningful green policies within your organisation. Engage actively with your customers – inspire them to adopt sustainable habits and participate in challenges that make a real environmental impact.

1-Launching new sustainability initiatives
Introducing new eco-friendly products or services: launch products or services that have a reduced environmental impact. Highlight the sustainable aspects of these offerings in your marketing campaigns.

Implementing internal green policies: Launch new sustainability policies within your organisation, such as reducing energy usage, minimising waste, or implementing a recycling program.

Interactive challenges: Create interactive challenges or campaigns that encourage customers to commit to sustainable practices. This could include a month-long challenge to reduce plastic usage, save energy, or use public transportation.

Incentivising sustainable actions: Offer incentives to customers who participate in sustainability challenges or who make eco-friendly purchases. This could include discounts, loyalty points, or rewards.

Track engagement and participation: Monitor customer engagement with your new initiatives and challenges. This includes measuring participation rates, social media engagement, and feedback received.

Make the most of the of sustainability momentum by launching comprehensive initiatives and integrating "green" practices across your organisation and customer base.

GENERATIVE AI CHEAT SHEET: PERFORMANCE

Month 10 is a time to summarise the year's achievements and show gratitude to clients and partners through year-end reviews, gifts, and appreciation events.

Prompt 1: "Analyse the performance data of your most recent marketing campaign, focusing on key metrics such as engagement rates, conversion rates, and ROI. Identify patterns and trends in the data, and provide a comprehensive report that highlights successes, areas for improvement, and actionable insights for future campaigns."
Application: Utilise Generative AI to analyse existing content performance and customer engagement data to inform the creation of new, optimised content.

Prompt 2: "Review and interpret customer feedback collected from various channels during our last campaign. Summarize the overall sentiment, key concerns, and praises. Extract actionable insights that can inform the refinement of our marketing messages, content strategy, and customer engagement practices."
Application: Leverage the power of Generative AI in predictive analytics to forecast the potential success of different campaign strategies.

Refine your prompting skills.
Clarify the purpose: if your task has a specific goal, such as persuading, informing, or entertaining, state this in your prompt. Understanding the purpose can significantly affect the response's tone and content.

PERSONAL BRAND: OPTIMISATION

This month is dedicated to utilising the power of data analytics and optimisation techniques to enhance your brand's online presence and engagement. Assess the impact of your efforts, understand the preferences and behaviours of your audience, and make informed adjustments to your strategies. Through a systematic approach to analysing performance, gathering feedback, conducting tests, and optimising digital assets, you're on the right path to grow your personal brand's effectiveness and reach.

Week 1: Analysing your personal brand's online performance
The month begins with a deep dive into the analytics of your personal brand's online performance. This involves utilising tools to track and analyse website traffic, social media engagement, content reach, and other key metrics. The goal is to gain insights into what's working well and what could be improved, identifying patterns and trends that can inform your future content and strategy decisions.

Week 2: Using feedback to improve your brand
Feedback is an invaluable resource for brand growth, offering direct insights into the perceptions and needs of your audience. The second week focuses on actively soliciting and analysing feedback from your followers, customers, and peers. This can involve surveys, comment sections, social media interactions, and other feedback channels.

Week 3: A/B testing for your personal branding strategies
Experimentation is key to optimising your personal branding efforts, and A/B testing offers a structured approach to understanding what resonates best with your audience. During the third week, you'll explore the process of conducting A/B tests on various elements of your brand's online presence, from email marketing campaigns to landing pages and social media posts.

Week 4: Optimising your website and social media profiles
This involves implementing the insights gained from analytics, feedback, and ensure consistency across your brand's online touchpoints. From refining your website's design and navigation to updating your social media bios and visuals, the focus is on making strategic adjustments that boost your brand's visibility, accessibility, and appeal to your target audience.

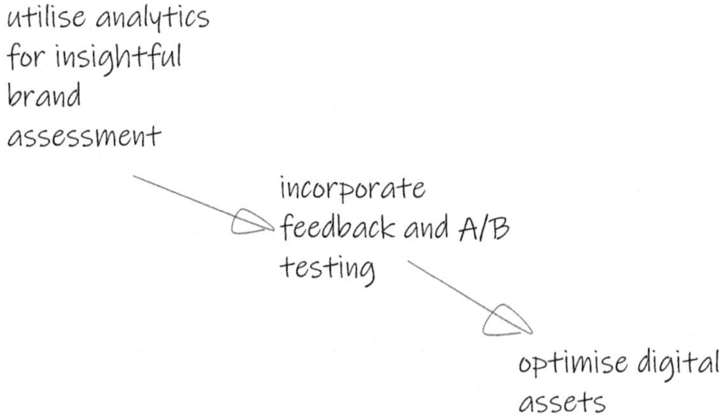

Analyse performance, embrace feedback, experiment with A/B testing and optimize your digital presence to ensure that your personal brand remains dynamic, relevant, and aligned with the evolving preferences of your audience.

MONTH 11

Must-read: **Contagious: How to build word of mouth in the digital age"** by Jonah Berger

Focus: understand how to make ideas and products go "viral".

ANALYSING AND OPTIMISING

This period is critical for dissecting the results of your major campaigns, understanding their impact, and refining your strategies for even greater success in the future.

Use predictive analytics to enhance optimisation. By examining past data and current market trends, predictive models can estimate future consumer behaviour, enabling you to predict changes in tastes and adapt your strategies accordingly. This active approach prepares you to keep up with the curve, making sure your marketing efforts are not just reactive but foresighted.

1– Segmentation

Divide your campaign data into segments based on different criteria such as demographics, location, or behaviour. This segmentation helps you to analyse more finely and identify what appealed to each segment and how. Adapting your future campaigns to better match the interests of these segments can greatly improve engagement and conversion rates.

2– A/B test

Take your analysis a step further by setting up A/B tests based on your findings. For example, if your data suggests certain types of content or calls to action (CTAs) performed better than others, test these elements in smaller, controlled campaigns to validate your insights. This method not only confirms your hypotheses but also refines your understanding of what works best for your audience.

GOOD TO KNOW

The process of analysing campaign performance should go beyond surface-level metrics. Analyse behavioural data, conversion paths, and customer feedback to get a comprehensive view of your campaign's effectiveness. This deeper understanding can reveal insights that significantly improve future ROI.

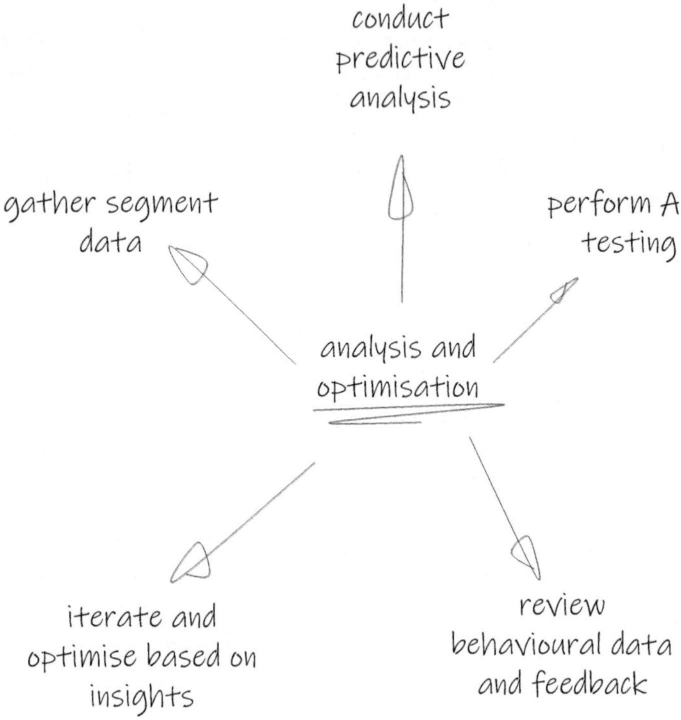

CTA: Review your campaign plans with a fresh perspective. Identify opportunities for enhanced engagement and pinpoint the data that will guide your optimisation efforts.

SUSTAINABLE MARKETING: RESPONSIBLE RELATIONSHIPS

This month invites a closer look at your supply chain. It's time to act in creating and keeping responsible relationships. Audit your suppliers, partner with ethically aligned businesses, and promote transparency in your supply chain. Your commitment to responsible relationships increases your brand's sustainability profile and contributes to a more ethical and environmentally friendly business ecosystem. The impact of your efforts will resonate far beyond your business it will strengthen your brand's commitment to a greener planet and to the community.

1-Strategies for building responsible relationships
Supplier sustainability audits: Conduct thorough audits of your suppliers to ensure they meet your sustainability standards. This includes evaluating their environmental practices, working conditions, and ethical standards.

Sustainability training and development: Offer training and resources to suppliers to help them improve their sustainability practices. This not only ensures compliance but also supports the overall sustainability ecosystem.

Supplier compliance rates: Monitor the compliance rates of your suppliers in meeting your sustainability criteria. Regular audits and assessments can help in tracking their adherence.

Sustainability improvements: Evaluate any improvements in sustainability metrics within your supply chain, such as reductions in carbon emissions or waste.

To do: Actively engage in building and maintaining responsible relationships.

GENERATIVE AI CHEAT SHEET: RETENTION

Month 11 focus is on the heart of business - nurturing and strengthening relationships. It's an important time for client retention and deepening bonds through feedback surveys and relationship management tools.

Prompt 1: "Explore strategies for strengthening client relationships and improving retention rates."
Application: Share insights on using client feedback surveys and relationship management tools to understand and serve clients better.

Prompt 2: "Discuss the long-term benefits of investing in client relationships for business growth and stability."
Application: Provide content, highlighting the importance of strong relationships in driving repeat business, referrals, and sustained growth.

Refine your prompting skills.
Use iterative refinement: Start with a broad prompt and refine your request based on ChatGPT's responses. This iterative approach can help zero in on the precise information or output you need.

PERSONAL BRAND: SCALING

Reaching a point where you're ready to scale is both exciting and daunting. To scale your personal brand, you need more than just a larger reach. You also need stronger relationships, wider impact, and higher quality content for your audience. This process demands careful planning, regularity, and a readiness to adapt. In this chapter, we'll look at a month-long strategy that helps you scale your personal brand efficiently, making sure that as your audience increases, so does your brand's core and value.

Week 1: Strengthening your foundation
Before scaling, it's important to verify your brand's foundation is solid. Revisit your brand's core message and values. Are they still aligned with the content you produce and the way you engage with your audience?

Week 2: Diversify your content strategy
With a solid foundation, it's time to focus on expanding your content's reach. Identify new content formats that you haven't explored yet but are popular among your target audience. This could be video content, podcasts, or live sessions.

Week 3: Forge strategic partnerships
Collaborations and partnerships can dramatically increase your brand's visibility and add value to your audience. List potential partners, influencers, or brands that align with your personal brand and have a substantial or highly engaged audience.

Week 4: Scaling through community building
The goal of scaling your personal brand is to increase numbers and to build a loyal community that engages with and advocates for your brand. Launch a community initiative that encourages interaction. This could be a challenge, a series of Q&A sessions, or a dedicated online forum where your audience can connect with each other. Actively participate in the community you're building. Engagement from your side can significantly boost the community's growth and the overall loyalty of your audience.

Systematically strengthen your brand's foundation, diversify your content, engage in strategic partnerships, and nurture a vibrant community, to scale your personal brand in a way that increases your influence and value proposition to your audience.

MONTH 12

Must-read: **"Can Marketing save the Planet"** by Michelle Carvill and Gemma Butler

Focus: 101 practical ways to use sustainable marketing as a force for good.

PLANNING AHEAD

Month 12 is a period of strategic thinking. The focus is in translating your learnings into a vision that aims higher and reaches further, setting new benchmarks for what your marketing efforts can achieve. This is the time to think strategically, plan, and prepare for a year of groundbreaking initiatives.

Stay abreast of the latest marketing technologies and platforms that can provide a competitive edge. Whether it's adopting new AI-driven analytics tools, exploring augmented reality in campaigns the willingness to experiment can lead to new successes.

1- Scenario-based planning

Engage in scenario-based planning to anticipate various market conditions and prepare multiple strategic responses. This approach helps in quickly adapting strategies based on actual market movements, ensuring your marketing efforts remain relevant and impactful.

2- Review milestones

Incorporate regular review milestones into your annual plan. These checkpoints are also opportunities to assess the effectiveness of your strategies and make necessary adjustments. By planning for these reviews, you ensure that your marketing strategy remains aligned with your business goals.

GOOD TO KNOW

Adopting a reflective practice is an acknowledgment that every marketing effort, regardless of its outcome, is a repository of invaluable lessons. The path to innovation and growth is paved with the learnings from our past actions. This period of reflection is our chance to distil wisdom from experience, ensuring that every step we take forward is informed, intentional, and imbued with the potential for transformation.

Engage with cross-functional teams to enrich your marketing strategy, cultivate a culture of collaboration and shared ownership.

SUSTAINABLE MARKETING: PREPARING FOR THE NEW FINANCIAL YEAR

Review your sustainability performance, set ambitious yet achievable goals for the new financial year, and bring your clients along on this journey. Your efforts in sustainable marketing are not just about business growth; they're about contributing to a greener, more sustainable world. Embrace this opportunity to make a difference, inspire change, and lead the way in sustainable business practices.

1-Reviewing the year's sustainability performance
Measuring impact: utilise key performance indicators (KPIs) to measure the impact of sustainability initiatives. This could include metrics like carbon footprint reduction, waste reduction, increases in sustainable product sales, or levels of customer engagement in sustainability campaigns.

Developing a strategic plan: create a detailed strategic plan that outlines the steps to achieve the set goals. This should include assigning responsibilities, setting timelines, and determining the resources required.

Marketing sustainability achievements and goals: use your marketing channels to highlight past achievements and future commitments in sustainability. Storytelling can be an effective tool to illustrate the journey and the impact of these efforts.

To-do: Review your sustainability performance and set ambitious yet achievable goals for the new financial year.

GENERATIVE AI CHEAT SHEET: WRAP-UP

Month 12 focus is on reflecting on the past financial year and preparing for the next. It's a time for comprehensive year-end reporting, tax preparation, and setting the stage for the upcoming financial year.

Prompt 1: "Discuss the key considerations and best practices for financial year wrap-up and reporting."
Application: Offer guidelines on effective year-end reporting, tax preparation, and analysis of the financial year's performance.

Prompt 2: "Highlight the importance of early preparation and strategic planning for the upcoming financial year."
Application: Share insights on the benefits of early planning, utilising wrap-up meetings to align strategies, and setting a strong foundation for the new financial year.

Refine your prompting skills.
Specify the desired structure: if you want your output to follow a certain format, such as a list, essay, or report, include it in your prompt. This can be important for tasks that need a specific style.

PERSONAL BRAND: REFLECTION

This month is about reviewing the progress made, understanding the impact of your efforts, and setting the stage for future growth. Through thoughtful analysis, feedback integration, goal setting, and strategic planning, you're not just concluding a year's journey but also paving the way for continued success.

Week 1: Conducting a comprehensive year-end review of your personal brand
Evaluate your achievements against the goals set at the year's start, analysing the strategies that worked and those that didn't, and assessing your brand's growth in visibility, engagement, and influence. Reflect on the milestones reached and the challenges faced, as this reflection is crucial for informed planning and improvement.

Week 2: Gathering and implementing year-end feedback
Feedback can significantly shape the trajectory of your personal brand. Actively seek feedback from your audience, peers, mentors, and collaborators. Utilise surveys, social media interactions, and direct conversations to gather insights into how your brand is perceived and the value it provides.

Week 3: Setting strategic goals for the next year
With a clear understanding of the past year's performance and armed with valuable feedback, the third week of Month twelve is about looking ahead and setting strategic goals for the coming year. These goals should be specific, measurable, achievable, relevant, and time- bound (SMART), aligned with your long-term vision for your personal brand. Consider new areas for growth, opportunities for engagement, and strategies to enhance your brand's visibility and impact.

Week 4: Developing a roadmap for continued personal branding success
Dedicate the last week of this month to turning your strategic goals into a tangible plan of action. Develop a roadmap for the upcoming year that outlines key initiatives, content strategies, marketing efforts, and milestones. This roadmap should serve as a guide for your personal branding activities, ensuring that you have a clear direction and focus for continuous growth and success.

performance review

-including metrics on social media engagement, website traffic, content reach, and any other relevant KPIs you've been tracking.

compare these figures against the goals you set at the beginning of the year.

feedback collection

-design and distribute surveys to your audience, and reach out directly to peers, mentors, and collaborators for their feedback.

compile the feedback received and analyse it for common themes and insights.

goal setting

-set SMART goals for your personal brand for the upcoming year. These goals should aim at addressing any identified gaps.

ensure each goal aligns with your overall vision for your personal brand.

20 TYPES OF MARKETING

1. C2B (Consumer-to-Business) Marketing:

In C2B, consumers offer products or services to businesses. This is common in crowdsourcing projects or affiliate marketing where consumers drive value to businesses.

2. C2C (Consumer-to-Consumer) Marketing:

This type involves transactions between consumers, often facilitated by third-party platforms like eBay or Etsy. It's common in marketplaces, online auctions, and classified advertisements.

3. B2G (Business-to-Government) Marketing:

B2G marketing involves selling products or services to government agencies or institutions. This often requires adherence to specific procurement processes and regulations.

4. B2E (Business-to-Employee) Marketing:

B2E focuses on providing products or services to the employees of a company, like internal software tools, employee benefits, or corporate training programs.

5. Social Media Marketing:

Utilises social media platforms to promote products or services. This type of marketing can cater to both B2C and B2B markets.

6. Influencer Marketing:

Involves partnering with influencers to promote products or services to their followers, commonly seen in B2C markets.

7. Content Marketing:

Focuses on creating and distributing valuable, relevant, and consistent content to attract and retain a clearly defined audience.

8. Affiliate Marketing:

Involves a business rewarding one or more affiliates for each visitor or customer brought by the affiliate's own marketing efforts.

9. Email Marketing:

Involves sending a commercial message, typically to a group of people, using email. It can be used in both B2B and B2C contexts.

10. Search Engine Marketing (SEM) and Search Engine Optimisation (SEO):

SEM involves promoting websites by increasing their visibility in search engine results pages primarily through paid advertising, while SEO focuses on optimising websites to rank higher in search engine results organically.

11. Green or Environmental Marketing:

Focuses on creating and selling products that are environmentally friendly, targeting consumers who are conscious of environmental issues.

12. Cause-Related Marketing:

A collaboration between a for-profit business and a non-profit organisation for mutual benefit, often leveraging the social causes to market products or services.

13. Experiential Marketing:

Focuses on creating experiences between brands and consumers, like events or interactive activities, to create a memorable impact.

14. Mobile Marketing:

Involves marketing on or with mobile devices, such as smartphones and tablets, often through apps, SMS, or mobile web browsing.

15. Viral Marketing:

Entails creating content or promotions that are so engaging that consumers will want to share them, leading to increased exposure and message spread.

16. Guerrilla Marketing:

Utilises unconventional and creative strategies to capture attention and engage consumers, often with limited budget resources. It's known for being surprising, witty, and memorable.

17. Direct Marketing:

Involves direct communication with targeted individual consumers to obtain an immediate response and cultivate lasting customer relationships.

18. Niche Marketing:

Targeting a specific, well-defined segment of the market. This type of marketing is often used by smaller companies with limited budgets.

19. Global Marketing:

Involves a company extending its marketing efforts beyond its home country and marketing to international customers.

20. Relationship Marketing:

Focuses on building stronger loyalty and long-term customer engagement rather than on immediate, short-term customer acquisition and individual sales.

MARKETING SCOPE
SUPPORT OR STRATEGIC FUNCTION

In some organisations marketing is still viewed as a mere support function, a useful but not critical part of the business strategy. This view, based on an old-fashioned idea of marketing's role, ignores the changes that marketing has experienced over time. Today, the marketing function goes beyond its previous limits, transforming into a vital, strategic factor that drives business growth and innovation.

In the not-so-distant past, marketing was considered a department that mainly focused on promotional activities, merch, and advertising. It was supposed to carry out the vision and strategy created by the 'central' functions of the business, such as operations, finance, and product development. This narrow view pushed marketing to the margins, failing to recognise its ability to impact and guide the strategic course of a company.

The digital revolution (and data analytics) has changed the business world and marketing must change with it. Marketing is now a power that connects different parts in this era of information and communication, blending creativity with analysis, and strategy with action.

However, there's more to be done. Many organisations claim that marketing is vital and fundamental, but marketers still struggle to get a seat at the table.

One of the main reasons marketing is seen as a mere support function is its historically vague scope. Unlike departments with clear responsibilities and metrics, such as sales or production, marketing's scope covers a wide range of activities from market research and brand management to customer engagement and digital campaigns. This wide scope, while a sign of marketing's adaptability, has made it difficult to measure its direct impact on a company's bottom line, leading to its underrating.

In addition, the "intangible" nature of many marketing outcomes - brand equity, customer loyalty, market influence, conversions - further complicates the attempt to quantify its value. As a result, marketing budgets are often the first to face cuts during financial downturns, reflecting a lingering perception of marketing as a dispensable, rather than essential, function.

However, I see a shift in perception.

Forward thinking business leaders are recognising that marketing is much more than a cost centre; it is a critical driver of revenue and long-term profitability. With its unique vantage point at the intersection of market trends, consumer behaviour, and technological innovation, marketing is uniquely positioned to identify new opportunities and steer strategic decisions. By using data analytics to anticipate market changes, and social media to interact with customers in real time, marketing is driving the business transformation of our times.

To solidify its role as a strategic powerhouse, it is important for marketing to clearly define and communicate its scope, objectives, and metrics. This involves setting quantifiable goals aligned with business objectives, employing robust analytics to measure performance, and demonstrating how marketing initiatives contribute to overall growth and profitability.

Not sure where to start? Here's some key areas that will help you define the scope of your marketing team:

-Understanding the market and clients.
Regularly conduct in-depth analysis to understand market trends, industry shifts, and emerging opportunities.
Client profiling: Develop detailed profiles of target clients, including their business needs, purchasing processes, and decision-making hierarchies.

-Brand positioning and messaging.
Define a clear brand identity that resonates with business clients, emphasising aspects like reliability, industry expertise, and service excellence.
Create messaging that addresses the specific needs, challenges, and pain points of the B2B audience.

-Product or service management.
Ensure that the products or services offered meet the highest standards and are tailored to the specific requirements of business clients.
Manage product or service portfolios to align with evolving market needs and client feedback.

-Lead generation and sales enablement
Implement targeted lead generation strategies, including content marketing, SEO, and strategic partnerships.
Equip the sales team with tools, materials, and training to effectively convert leads into clients.

-Relationship building and account management
Focus on building strong, long-term relationships with clients through regular communication, personalised service, and understanding of their

evolving business needs.
Implement account management practices that ensure client satisfaction, retention, and opportunities for upselling or cross-selling.

-Data-driven decision making
Utilise CRM systems and marketing analytics tools to gather data on client interactions, campaign performance, and market trends.
Analyse data to make informed decisions, measure ROI, and continually refine marketing strategies.

-Content and communication strategy
Develop educational, informative content that establishes the company as a thought leader and helps clients make informed decisions.
Utilise multiple channels (like email marketing, social media, blogs, and webinars) to engage with the B2B audience and provide valuable insights.

-Feedback and continuous improvement
Regularly seek feedback from clients to understand their experiences, expectations, and areas for improvement.
Encourage a culture of constant learning, using customer feedback and market data to improve products, services, and customer experiences.

ACCESSIBILITY

Accessibility in marketing involves the commitment to creating marketing materials, campaigns, and experiences that are inclusive and accessible to all individuals, including those with disabilities. This approach not only aligns with legal obligations under UK laws but also reflects a broader understanding of diversity in consumer needs and preferences.

Here's what you should know about accessibility in marketing:

Legal framework and compliance: In the UK, compliance with laws such as the Equality Act 2010 is crucial. This Act requires businesses to make reasonable adjustments to avoid discriminating against individuals with disabilities. Additionally, adhering to global web accessibility standards like the Web Content Accessibility Guidelines (WCAG) guarantees that digital content is accessible to all users.

Inclusive and universal design: This involves creating marketing materials (websites, apps, videos, digital content) that are accessible to everyone, including people with visual, auditory, motor, and cognitive disabilities. Practical steps include providing alternative text for images, ensuring sufficient colour contrast, offering subtitles for videos, and making websites navigable by keyboard and screen readers.

Ethical marketing and Corporate Social Responsibility (CSR): Accessible marketing in the UK is also about demonstrating empathy and a commitment to ethical marketing. Companies that prioritise accessibility are seen as socially responsible and are likely to enjoy enhanced brand perception and customer loyalty.

User feedback and continuous improvement: Engaging with users, especially those with disabilities, and incorporating their feedback is crucial. Accessibility should be viewed as a dynamic, ongoing process that evolves with changing user needs and technological advancements.

Leveraging technology for accessibility: Utilising the latest technology, including AI, to create personalised user experiences and improve accessibility features, such as voice recognition, automatic alt text for images, and advanced screen reader capabilities, can significantly enhance the inclusivity of marketing efforts.

Training and awareness: Ensuring that staff are trained in accessibility principles and are aware of the importance of inclusion. This can be facilitated through regular training sessions and by fostering a workplace culture where accessibility is a shared value.

Enhancing brand image: In the UK, where consumers are increasingly aware of and value corporate ethics, accessible marketing can significantly boost a company's image and reputation. It showcases the company's commitment to inclusivity and its dedication to serving the entire community, aligning with the values of diversity and inclusion.

MARKETING 101

METHODOLOGIES

SWOT ANALYSIS

SWOT Analysis (Strengths, Weaknesses, Opportunities, Threats) is a strategic planning tool used to identify and analyse the internal strengths and weaknesses of a business, as well as external opportunities and threats. It helps in crafting strategies that align a company's resources and capabilities with the competitive environment.

strengths	weaknesses	opportunities	threats
internal, positive factors	internal, negative factors	external, positive factors	external, negative factors

So what?

Maximise: (Strengths x Opportunities) - How can strengths be used to maximise opportunities?

Minimise: (Weaknesses x Threats) - How can weaknesses be minimised to avoid threats?

Capitalise: (Strengths x Threats) - How can strengths be used to mitigate or capitalise on threats?

Improve: (Weaknesses x Opportunities) - How can weaknesses be improved to take advantage of opportunities?

PORTER'S 5 FORCES

1 - Threat of new entrants
This force examines how easy or difficult it is for competitors to join the marketplace.

2 - Bargaining power of suppliers
This force looks at the power suppliers must drive up the prices of your inputs.

3 - Bargaining power of buyers
This force analyses how much pressure customers can place on your business.

4 - Threat of substitute products or services
This force considers the likelihood and capability of customers switching to a substitute product or service.

5 - Competitive rivalry among existing competitors
This force examines the intensity of competition in the marketplace.

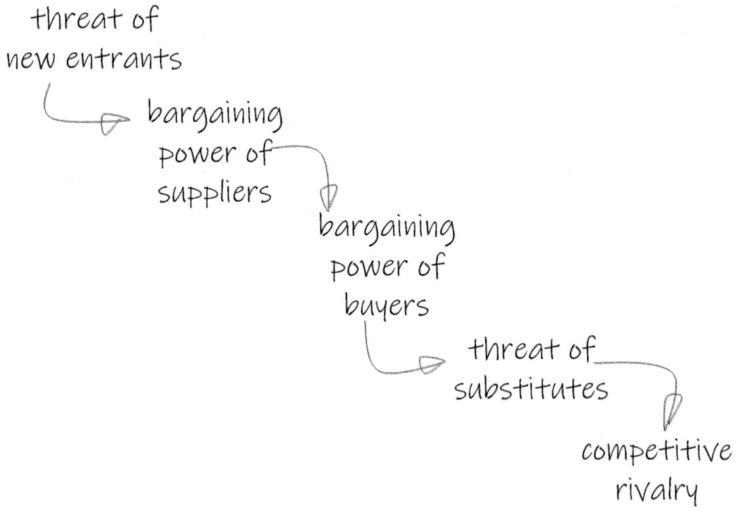

So what?
Leverage Weak Forces: If certain forces are weak (e.g., low bargaining power of suppliers), consider how you can leverage this to your advantage (e.g., negotiate better terms).

Mitigate Strong Forces: If certain forces are strong (e.g., high threat of new entrants), develop strategies to mitigate their impact (e.g., strengthen brand loyalty, invest in technology).

THE 4 P'S OF MARKETING

1. Product
Description: The goods or services that a business offers to meet the needs of its customers.

2. Price
Description: The amount of money customers must pay to acquire the product or service.

3. Place (Distribution)
Description: How the product or service is delivered to the customer. This includes the locations where the product is sold and the distribution channels used.

4. Promotion
Description: The activities undertaken to make customers aware of the product or service, including advertising, sales promotions, public relations, and personal selling.

product	price	place	promotion
evaluate how well your product meets the needs of your target market	assess how your pricing strategy aligns with market expectations and your overall business strategy	determine the effectiveness of your distribution channels in reaching your target market	evaluate the impact of your promotional activities on market awareness and sales

So what?
Action Steps: Outline specific, actionable steps for each 'P.'

Responsibilities: Assign team members responsible for implementing actions in each area.

Review and Optimise: Regularly review performance against your strategic goals and optimise your 4 Ps as needed.

THE STP MODEL

1. Segmentation
Divide the broader market into smaller, distinct groups based on common characteristics. In B2B markets, segmentation is often based on factors like industry, company size, geographic location, or specific needs.

2. Targeting
Evaluate each market segment's attractiveness and select one or more segments to focus on. In B2B marketing, targeting decisions are often based on factors like market potential, competition, and alignment with the company's resources and expertise.

3. Positioning
Define how you want the market to perceive your product or service relative to competitors. Positioning involves creating a unique, compelling image of the product in the customer's mind.

segmentatio	targeting	positioning
identify variables for segmentatio n, analyse segments	evaluate segment attractivene ss, select target segments	define positioning strategy, create a positioning statement

So what?
Marketing mix development: Develop your marketing mix (4 Ps) to support the positioning strategy for each target segment.

Monitor and adjust: Regularly review market feedback, sales data, and other performance indicators. Be prepared to adjust your segmentation, targeting, or positioning strategies based on this feedback.

THE AIDA MODEL

1. Attention (Awareness)
Capturing the potential customer's attention is the first step. The goal is to make the consumer aware of your brand or product.

2. Interest
Once you have the consumer's attention, the next step is to engage their interest by focusing on how your product or service meets their needs or desires.

3. Desire
Interest evolves into desire when the consumer starts to want the product or service. This stage is about creating an emotional connection and convincing the consumer that your product will satisfy their needs or desires.

4. Action
The final stage involves encouraging the consumer to take action – usually to make a purchase. However, the action could also be other forms of conversion, such as signing up for a newsletter or sharing content on social media.

attentio	interest	desire	action
assess the reach and effectivenes s of your attention-grabbing efforts	evaluate the engagement and depth of interaction with your content or ads	determine the emotional connection and intent to purchase	track the conversion rate and other actions taken

So what?
Action Steps: Outline specific, actionable steps for each stage of AIDA.

Collect Feedback: Gather continuous feedback at each stage to understand how your marketing efforts are being perceived and what impact they are having.

Refine AIDA Strategy: Use the feedback to refine your strategies and tactics at each stage of AIDA to better meet the needs and expectations of your audience.

CONSUMER DECISION JOURNEY

1. Initial consideration
The consumer becomes aware of a set of brands or products as potential options to fulfil their needs, often influenced by advertising, word of mouth, or previous experiences.

2. Active evaluation (Research and Shopping)
The consumer actively gathers information, researches options, and evaluates the choices. This stage is heavily influenced by marketing touchpoints, reviews, and comparison shopping.

3. Closure (Purchase)
The consumer makes their purchase decision and completes the transaction. This stage can be influenced by the shopping experience, pricing, promotions, and the ease of purchase.

4. Post-purchase experience
After purchasing, the consumer builds expectations based on their experience with the product or service, which influences their future purchase decisions and their likelihood of recommending the brand to others.

5. Loyalty loop
For consumers who have a strong, positive post-purchase experience, the journey can lead to a loyalty loop, where the consumer skips or shortens the initial consideration and active evaluation stages and repeatedly purchases from the brand.

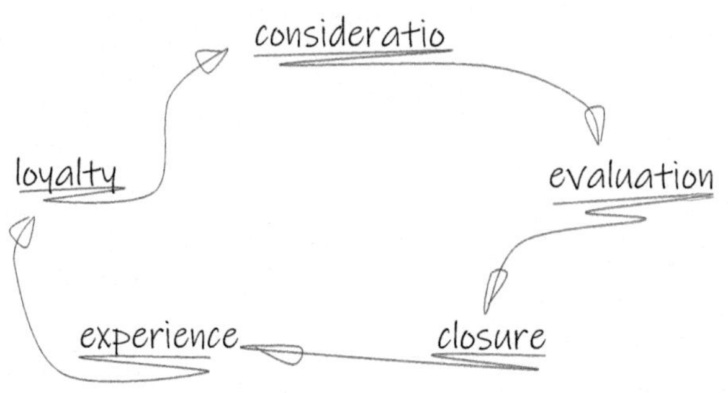

So what?
Action steps: Outline specific, actionable steps for each stage of the CDJ.

Review and optimise: Regularly review performance against your CDJ goals and optimise your efforts as needed.

Collect feedback: Gather continuous feedback at each stage to understand how your marketing efforts are perceived and what impact they are having.

Refine CDJ strategy: Use the feedback to refine your strategies and tactics at each stage of the CDJ to better meet the needs and expectations of your audience.

CONSUMER DECISION MAPPING

1. Awareness Stage
The customer becomes aware of your brand or product. This could be through advertising, word of mouth, or social media.

2. Consideration Stage
The customer starts considering your product by seeking more information, reading reviews, or comparing with other products.

3. Purchase Stage
The customer decides to purchase the product. The ease of the purchasing process can significantly impact their experience.

4. Retention Stage
After the purchase, the customer's post-purchase experience with the product and the brand can influence their loyalty and likelihood of making future purchases.

5. Advocacy Stage
A positive overall experience can turn customers into brand advocates. They may leave positive reviews, recommend the product to friends, or engage with the brand on social media.

before creating a CJM you should:

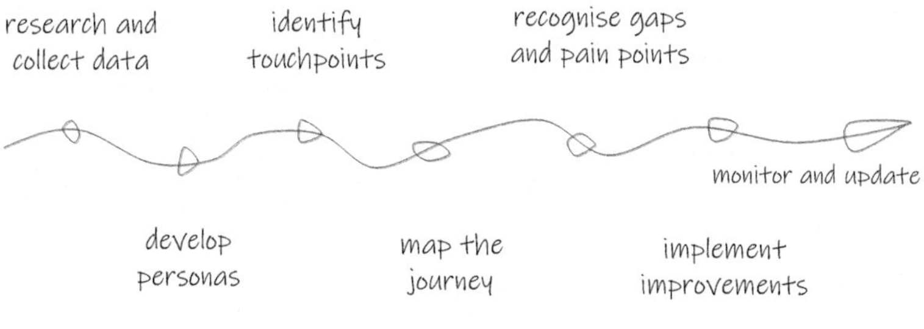

So what?

Action steps: Outline specific, actionable steps for each stage of the Customer Journey.

Responsibilities: Assign team members responsible for implementing actions at each stage.

Review and optimise: Regularly review performance against your customer journey goals and optimise your efforts as needed.

Collect feedback: Gather continuous feedback at each stage to understand how your efforts are perceived and what impact they are having.

Refine strategy: Use the feedback to refine your strategies and tactics at each stage of the Customer Journey to better meet the needs and expectations of your audience.

MARKETING IN NUMBERS

METRICS – THE REALITY OF INSIGHT

Marketing metrics, from Return on Investment (ROI) to Customer Lifetime Value (CLV), and my favourite Marketing Influenced Revenue (MIR), promise a veneer of precision. However, their true value isn't in the precision they offer, but in the insights they deliver.

Incorporating realistic metrics into a marketing strategy allows for data-driven decision-making, helping to allocate resources effectively and optimise marketing efforts. It's important to use a combination of metrics to get a comprehensive view of your marketing performance.

Return on Investment (ROI):
Definition: Measures the profitability of a marketing campaign by comparing the revenue it generates to the cost of the campaign.

Example: If you spend £10,000 on a marketing campaign and generate £50,000 in sales from that campaign, the ROI would be (50,000 - 10,000) / 10,000 = 4 or 400%.
Reference: Kotler, P., & Keller, K. L. (2016). Marketing Management (15th ed.). Pearson Education, Inc.

Customer Acquisition Cost (CAC):
Definition: Calculates the total cost of acquiring a new customer, including all marketing and sales expenses.

Example: If you spend £5,000 on marketing and sales and acquire 100 new customers, the CAC would be 5,000 / 100 = £50 per customer.
Reference: Blattberg, R. C., & Deighton, J. (1996). Manage Marketing by the Customer Equity Test. Harvard Business Review.

Customer Lifetime Value (CLV):
Definition: Estimates the total revenue a business can reasonably expect from a single customer account throughout the business relationship.

Example: If a customer spends £1,000 annually, stays with the company for an average of 10 years, and the discount rate is 10%, the CLV would be £1,000 * (1 - (1 / (1 + 0.1)^10)) / 0.1 = £6,144.57.
Reference: Gupta, S., Lehmann, D. R., & Stuart, J. A. (2004). Valuing Customers. Journal of Marketing Research.

Conversion Rate:
Definition: Measures the percentage of users who take a desired action out of the total number of users.

Example: If 1,000 visitors come to your landing page and 100 of them fill out the contact form, the conversion rate would be 100 / 1,000 = 10%.
Reference: Eisenberg, B., Quarto-von Tivadar, J., & Davis, L. T. (2006). Call to Action: Secret Formulas to Improve Online Results. Thomas Nelson Inc.

Lead Conversion Rate:
Definition: Calculates the percentage of leads that become paying customers.

Example: If you generate 200 leads and 20 of them become customers, the lead conversion rate would be 20 / 200 = 10%.
Reference: Hughes, A. M. (2005). Strategic Database Marketing. McGraw-Hill.

Net Promoter Score (NPS):
Definition: Measures customer satisfaction and loyalty by asking customers how likely they are to recommend the business to others.

Example: After surveying, if 70% of respondents are promoters (score 9-10), 10% are detractors (score 0-6), the NPS would be 70 - 10 = 60.
Reference: Reichheld, F. F. (2003). The One Number You Need to Grow. Harvard Business Review.

Click-Through Rate (CTR):
Definition: The percentage of people who click on a link out of the total number of people who see the link.

Example: If your email campaign is viewed by 1,000 people and 50 people click on the link, the CTR would be 50 / 1,000 = 5%.
Reference: Chaffey, D., & Ellis-Chadwick, F. (2019). Digital Marketing. Pearson Education Limited.

Marketing Influenced Revenue:

The concept of Marketing Influenced Revenue particularly resonates with me. It acknowledges the subtle yet significant touchpoints of marketing throughout the customer journey.

In many large B2B organisations, marketing and sales operate in parallel universes; they work alongside each other often siloed in their own delivery objectives. This separation makes calculating the return on investment (ROI) a somewhat fictitious task, as marketing is not involved in the entire sales cycle and typically doesn't know when the cycle concludes or when new contracts are secured. However, if we shift the focus to 'marketing influenced revenue' we will end up with a more realistic and, perhaps, more accurate perspective.

To start it's important to define "marketing-influenced revenue." In essence, it should include any sales where the prospect has interacted with marketing at any point during the decision-making process. This can range from initial awareness, through consideration, and up to the final decision-making stage. Some organisations might opt for a narrower definition, such as considering only those leads that originated directly from marketing efforts.

What can effectively be tracked and measured?

Implement robust systems to track previously defined interactions a prospect has with marketing. This includes monitoring website visits, content downloads, social media engagements, attendance at marketing events, or interactions with email campaigns, etc. Leverage Customer Relationship Management (CRM) systems and marketing automation tools are instrumental for this purpose. Then select a realistic attribution model. Attribution models are essentially a set of rules that determine how credit for sales and conversions is assigned to touchpoints in the customer journey.

Here's a few examples:

- First Touch Attribution: Where 100% of the credit goes to the initial interaction.
- Last Touch Attribution: Where the final interaction before the sale gets 100% of the credit.
- Linear Attribution: Where credit is evenly split among all interactions.
- Time Decay Attribution: Where more credit is given to interactions that occur closer in time to the sale.

- Position-Based Attribution: Where 40% of the credit is allocated to both the first and last interactions, with the remaining 20% distributed evenly among the middle interactions.

Calculating Marketing Influenced Revenue in a B2B Context

Let's take a hypothetical B2B company, "Tech Solutions Inc.", that sells enterprise software solutions. Here's how they might calculate their marketing-influenced revenue using the attribution model:

Track interactions and collect data:

- Tech Solutions Inc. uses a CRM system to track all interactions with potential and existing clients.
    - They monitor various touchpoints, including website visits, content downloads, webinar attendance, email engagement, and interactions at trade shows.

- Set an attribution model:
    - Given the complex nature of their sales cycles, Tech Solutions Inc. opts for a linear attribution model, where every touchpoint in the customer journey is given equal credit for the sale.

- Analyse sales data:
    - Consider a scenario where Tech Solutions Inc. closed a deal worth £100,000.
    - Throughout the sales process, the client had 10 significant interactions with Tech Solutions Inc.'s marketing materials and sales team.

- Apply the attribution model:
    - With a linear model, each touchpoint gets equal credit. So, each interaction is worth 10% of the deal value in terms of influencing the sale.
    - If 6 out of these 10 interactions were marketing efforts (like attending a webinar, downloading whitepapers, or engaging with marketing emails), then marketing gets credit for 60% of the deal.

- Calculate marketing influenced revenue (MIR):

    - The total value of the deal is £100,000.
    - Marketing is attributed with 60% influence on this deal.
    - So, marketing-influenced revenue for this deal would be 60% of £100,000, which is £60,000.

- Aggregate and analyse:
    - Tech Solutions Inc. would aggregate this data over all deals in each period to understand the overall impact of marketing on revenue.
    - This helps in analysing the investment of different marketing strategies and guides future budget allocations.

In a B2B context, calculating marketing-influenced revenue can be complex due to longer sales cycles and the often-multifaceted nature of decision-making processes. Before developing any plans, here's some key points to consider:

Complex Sales Processes: In B2B, the interaction between marketing and sales is often intricate. Sales might take months or even years, with numerous interactions and stakeholders involved.

Choosing the Right Model: The choice of attribution model can significantly affect the calculated influence of marketing. It's important to choose a realistic and measurable model that aligns with your sales process and business objectives.

Continuous Refinement: Regularly review and adjust your approach based on performance data. What works for one product, service, or market segment might not work for another.

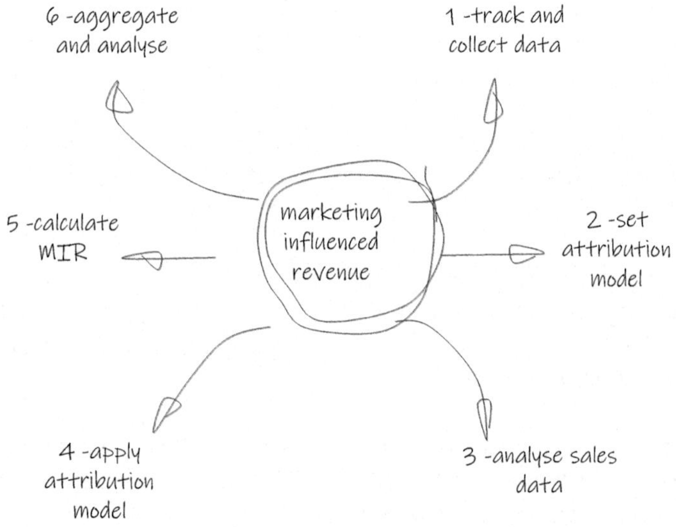
6 -aggregate and analyse
1 -track and collect data
marketing influenced revenue
5 -calculate MIR
2 -set attribution model
4 -apply attribution model
3 -analyse sales data

MARKETING LIFECYCLE

B2B MARKETING LIFECYCLE

The B2B marketing lifecycle includes a series of steps that are not purely transactional but transformational. It involves a meticulous process of identifying and understanding the needs and challenges of businesses, and then, with a blend of strategic acumen and creative flair, addressing these needs in a manner that not only solves problems but also adds value. Identifying each phase, from the initial market research to the final stages of customer advocacy, is interconnected and integral.

1. Market research and analysis
Duration: Ongoing, with intense periods at the start and at regular intervals.

Activity: Understand the market, competitors, and customer needs. Identify your target audience, their pain points, and decision-making processes.

Example: A SaaS company conducts surveys and focus groups to understand the challenges businesses face in managing remote teams.

Recommendation: Invest in quality research. Use tools like SWOT analysis to understand your position in the market.

2. Branding and positioning
Duration: Initial intense period, then ongoing maintenance.
Activity: Develop a strong brand identity and position your product or service to meet the identified needs of your target market.

Example: A cybersecurity firm positions itself as the most reliable solution for large enterprises by showcasing its success stories and testimonials.

Recommendation: Ensure your branding resonates with your target audience's values and your unique selling propositions (USPs) are clear.

3. Lead generation
Duration: Ongoing, as long as the business operates.
Activity: Use various channels like content marketing, SEO, PPC, and trade shows to generate interest and capture leads.

Example: A B2B manufacturing company uses LinkedIn ads targeting specific industries to generate leads.

Recommendation: Diversify your lead generation channels and consistently analyse the performance of each channel.

4. Lead nurturing
Duration: Weeks to months, depending on the sales cycle and the product complexity.

Activity: Engage with leads through email marketing, educational content, webinars, and personalized follow-ups to move them down the sales funnel.

Example: An IT service provider sends a series of educational emails about the latest industry trends and how their services can address the current market needs.

Recommendation: Personalize your communication. Understand the lead's position in the buying cycle and provide relevant content.

5. Sales conversion
Duration: Highly variable, from months to over a year.

Activity: Work closely with the sales team to convert qualified leads into customers. This involves product demos, proposal submissions, and negotiation.

Example: A commercial construction equipment supplier conducts on-site demos and customizes offers based on the specific needs of the business.

Recommendation: Ensure your sales team is well-equipped with product knowledge and has all the necessary tools to address potential customer objections.

6. Customer retention and growth
Duration: Indefinite, as long as the customer relationship lasts.

Activity: Provide excellent after-sales service, seek customer feedback, and offer tailored solutions to turn new customers into repeat buyers.

Example: A B2B software company offers regular training sessions and feature updates to ensure customers are getting the most out of the product.

Recommendation: Focus on building long-term relationships. Understand your customers' evolving needs and adapt your services accordingly.

7. Advocacy and referral
Duration: Indefinite, leveraging satisfied customers.

Activity: Encourage satisfied customers to become brand advocates. Implement referral programs to incentivize customers to bring new leads.

Example: A consulting firm creates a referral program that rewards existing clients with discounts or additional services for every successful referral.

Recommendation: Actively seek testimonials and case studies. Make it easy and rewarding for clients to refer new business to you.

The B2B marketing lifecycle is a continuous process with a duration that varies depending on the industry, product complexity, and market dynamics. It requires a strategic approach at each stage, focusing on understanding customer needs, building strong relationships, and continuously adapting to market changes.

Reference: Kotler, P., & Keller, K. L. (2016). Marketing Management (15th ed.). Pearson Education, Inc.

B2C MARKETING LIFECYCLE

The B2C (Business-to-Consumer) marketing lifecycle is a dynamic process that revolves around directly reaching and engaging consumers, influencing their purchasing decisions, and fostering loyalty. Compared to the B2B cycle, the B2C lifecycle is typically shorter, more transactional, and often driven by emotional decision-making.

1. Awareness
Duration: Short-term, ongoing efforts.

Activity: Introduce your brand and products to potential customers through advertising, social media, content marketing, and public relations.

Example: A clothing brand uses targeted social media ads to reach potential customers interested in sustainable fashion.

Recommendation: Use eye-catching, memorable messaging that resonates with the target audience's interests and values.

2. Consideration
Duration: Short to medium-term, depending on the product complexity and purchase frequency.

Activity: Engage interested consumers by providing detailed information about your products or services, showcasing benefits, and differentiating from competitors.

Example: A smartphone company releases comparison videos highlighting the superior features of its latest model compared to competitors.

Recommendation: Provide clear, concise, and compelling content that addresses consumer questions and showcases your unique selling proposition.

3. Purchase
Duration: Typically short-term, with the aim of making this stage as

seamless as possible.

Activity: Convert interest into sales through an optimized purchasing process, attractive offers, and strong calls to action.

Example: An online retailer offers a limited-time discount code, along with free next-day delivery, to encourage immediate purchases.

Recommendation: Ensure a smooth, hassle-free purchasing experience with multiple payment options and clear, reassuring communication about shipping and returns.

4. Retention
Duration: Long-term, ongoing efforts.

Activity: Foster customer loyalty and repeat purchases through excellent customer service, loyalty programs, and regular engagement via email marketing or social media.

Example: A beauty brand creates a loyalty program that rewards customers with points for each purchase, redeemable for discounts on future orders.

Recommendation: Continuously engage with customers post-purchase, seek feedback, and offer personalized recommendations or rewards to encourage repeat business.

5. Advocacy
Duration: Long-term, evolving with customer relationship.

Activity: Encourage satisfied customers to become brand advocates, sharing their positive experiences through reviews, testimonials, or word-of-mouth referrals.

Example: A fitness equipment brand encourages customers to share their workout

Reference: Kotler, P., & Keller, K. L. (2016). Marketing Management (15th ed.). Pearson Education, Inc.

MARKETING PLAN

Creating a comprehensive B2B marketing plan involves a structured approach, focusing on understanding the target market, defining objectives, and outlining strategies and tactics to achieve these goals. If you are a team of one, you must keep it simple. Discuss what's important to the organisation and keep the marketing plan a live and dynamic document. The marketing plan touchpoints below will help you define a clear outline of the marketing efforts and set specific objectives. This focus helps in aligning marketing strategies with business goals, ensuring that all marketing activities contribute to the overall objectives of the company. And it will also help the organisation to understand the time and effort needed to execute this plan.

A marketing plan will provide the information needed to support discussions around efficient allocation of resources - time, manpower, and budget - by prioritising marketing activities based on their potential impact.

1. Executive summary

Purpose: Summarise the main goals and the overarching strategy of the plan.

2. Market analysis

Industry overview: Describe the current state of the industry, trends, and outlook.

Competitor analysis: Identify key competitors, their market position, strengths, and weaknesses.

SWOT analysis: Outline your company's Strengths, Weaknesses, Opportunities, and Threats.

3. Target market and customer insights

Market segmentation: Segment the market based on industries, company size, or other relevant criteria.

Buyer personas: Develop detailed profiles of the decision-makers and influencers in the purchasing process.

Customer needs and pain points: List the needs, challenges, and pain points of your target customers.

4. Marketing goals and objectives

SMART goals: Set Specific, Measurable, Achievable, Relevant, and Time-bound goals aligned with the company's overall objectives.

5. Marketing strategies and tactics

Product/Service strategy: Define how your products or services meet the specific needs of your B2B clients.

Pricing strategy: Outline your pricing model, considering factors like cost, competition, and perceived value.

Distribution/Place strategy: Describe how and where your clients will buy your products or services.

Promotion strategy: Detail the promotional activities to reach and engage your target audience.

Include:

- Content marketing: Develop valuable and relevant content tailored to your buyer personas at different stages of the buyer's journey.
- Digital marketing: Utilise SEO, PPC, email marketing, and social media to generate leads and build brand awareness.
- Event marketing: Participate in or host industry events, webinars, or workshops to engage directly with potential clients.
- Public relations: Establish your company as a thought leader through press releases, articles, and industry reports.
- Sales enablement: Equip your sales team with the necessary tools, materials, and training.

6. Implementation plan

Action plan: Create a detailed list of actions, responsible persons, deadlines, and resources required.

Timeline: Develop a timeline with key milestones and checkpoints.

7. Budget

Budget allocation: Allocate budget to different marketing activities based on their expected ROI.

Cost analysis: Provide a detailed breakdown of all costs involved in the marketing activities.

8. Performance metrics and KPIs

Lead generation: Number of leads generated.

Conversion rates: Percentage of leads converted to customers.

Customer acquisition Cost (CAC).

Customer lifetime value (CLV).

ROI or MIR (Marketing Influenced Revenue).

Engagement metrics: Website traffic, social media engagement, content download.

9. Review and optimisation

Feedback mechanisms: Establish channels for collecting customer and team feedback.

Performance review: Regularly review the performance against KPIs.

Optimisation: Continuously optimise the marketing strategies based on performance data and feedback.

MARKETING TOOLKIT

A marketing toolkit is a collection of resources, templates, guidelines, and tools that streamline and guide the marketing efforts of a business. It's designed to ensure consistency, efficiency, and effectiveness in all marketing activities, aligning them with the brand's identity and objectives. The toolkit serves as a central repository that can be accessed by various team members, ensuring that everyone is on the same page and equipped with the necessary tools to execute their tasks. The marketing toolkit is the foundation of your brand strategy and business development, here's why:

Consistency: Ensures that all marketing materials and messages are consistent with the brand's voice, values, and visual identity, which is crucial for building brand recognition and trust.

Efficiency: Saves time and resources by providing ready-to-use templates and guidelines, reducing the need to create everything from scratch for each new campaign or project.

Alignment: Helps align marketing efforts with the overall business strategy, ensuring that all activities contribute to the broader business objectives.

Scalability: Enables businesses to scale their marketing efforts more easily, as the toolkit provides a framework that can be used across various campaigns and platforms.

Measurement: Includes tools and guidelines for tracking and analysing the performance of marketing activities, enabling continuous improvement.

How to create a marketing toolkit?

Define your brand guidelines:
- Include your brand's mission, vision, values, and personality.
- Detail the visual elements of your brand, such as logos, colour schemes, typography, and imagery guidelines.
- Provide examples of the tone of voice and messaging style for written content.

Compile key marketing templates and documents:
- Create templates for commonly used marketing materials, such as brochures, business cards, email newsletters, and social media posts.
- Include content calendars, project timelines, and budget sheets to help plan and track marketing activities.

Incorporate essential tools and software:
- List the tools and software used for various marketing activities, such as social media management, email marketing, CRM, and analytics.
- Provide access information and basic instructions or links to training resources for each tool.

Establish performance metrics and reporting guidelines:
- Define key performance indicators (KPIs) for different marketing activities.
- Include templates or tools for reporting and analysing marketing performance.

Provide training resources and best practices:
- Include guidelines, best practices, and tips for effective marketing practices.
- Provide access to training resources, webinars, or workshops to help team members develop their marketing skills.

Ensure accessibility and regular updates:
- Make sure the toolkit is easily accessible to all team members, preferably in a digital format that can be regularly updated.
- Schedule regular reviews of the toolkit to ensure that it remains up-to-date and relevant

Marketing toolkit

01
brand guidelines

logo, colour pallet (CMYK, RGB, HEX), typography (font styles, sizes, and spacing), imagery, tone of voice, brand applications, legal and copyright guidelines

02
templates

emails, brochures, presentations, business cards, proposals, social media

03
tools and software

CRM, CMS, email marketing, social media management, SEO, PPC, analytics and data visualisation, graphic design and video editing, project management and collaboration tools

04
metrics

profitability, acquisition, conversion rates, customer lifetime value, lead-to-customer ratio, social media, web, and email marketing

05
training and resources

guidelines, best practices, needs assessment, workshops, mentorship, coaching, feedback and continuous improvement

06
accessibility

centralised repository, standardised formats, structure and labelling, mobile accessibility

audit and update

EVENT MARKETING

Event marketing is an invaluable avenue for lead generation and data collection. It offers a unique platform for direct engagement with audiences, building personal connections, and brand loyalty. Events bring a brand to life, allowing business and organisations to showcase their products, services, and values in a live, interactive environment.

In addition, events allow businesses to gather real-time feedback and insights about their target audience, enabling them to tailor their offerings and marketing strategies more effectively. The immediacy of face-to-face interaction also accelerates the sales cycle, turning prospects into customers more swiftly compared to other marketing channels.

Event marketing also plays an important role in creating content and buzz on social media platforms, amplifying a brand's reach and engagement. Live events can be leveraged for content before, during, and after the actual event, extending the lifecycle of the marketing campaign and maximising return on investment.

Marketing events can follow many different frameworks, here's a structured approach to o developing an event marketing framework:

1. Define event objectives
Purpose and goals: Clearly define what you want to achieve with the event (e.g., brand awareness, lead generation, customer engagement).

2. Understand your audience
Target audience: Identify and understand the demographics, interests, and behaviour of your potential attendees.
Buyer personas: Create detailed profiles for different segments of your target audience.

3. Develop a Unique Value Proposition (UVP)
Event messaging: Develop a clear and compelling message that highlights the unique benefits and experiences the event offers.

4. Choose the right type and format
Event Type: Decide whether the event will be a webinar, workshop, conference, or another format.
Event Format: Determine if the event will be in-person, virtual, or hybrid, based on your audience's preferences and logistical considerations.

5. Develop a multi-channel communications plan
Promotional channels: Utilise a mix of channels suited to your audience, such as email, social media, content marketing, and partnerships.
Timeline: Create a detailed timeline for promotional activities, building momentum as the event date approaches.

6. Engage and mobilise attendees
Engagement strategies: Implement strategies to engage attendees before, during, and after the event (e.g., interactive sessions, networking opportunities, social media engagement).
Call-to-Action: Ensure every promotional piece includes a clear call-to-action (e.g., register, learn more, visit a booth).

7. Leverage event technology
Registration and management tools: Use event management software for registrations, ticketing, and attendee tracking.
Engagement tools: Incorporate tools for live polling, Q&A sessions, or virtual networking to enhance participant engagement.

8. Partner and sponsor outreach
Strategic partnerships: Collaborate with industry partners, influencers, or sponsors to expand your reach and add credibility to your event.

9. Measure performance and gather insights
Key Performance Indicators (KPIs): Establish KPIs to measure the success of your event (e.g., number of registrations, attendee satisfaction, leads generated).
Feedback and surveys: Collect attendee feedback to gain insights into their experience and gather data for improving future events.

10. Post-event follow-up
Engagement: Keep the conversation going with follow-up content, thank you messages, and calls to action for future engagement.
Lead nurturing: Incorporate leads into your CRM and initiate nurturing campaigns to convert prospects into customers.

MARKETING LINGO

Above the Line (ATL): Traditional mass media marketing aimed at a broad audience, usually through mediums like TV, radio, and print.

Below the Line (BTL): More direct and targeted marketing strategies, such as direct mail, email marketing, and trade shows.

Conversion Rate: The percentage of visitors who take a desired action, like making a purchase or filling out a form.

Customer Acquisition Cost (CAC): The cost associated with acquiring a new customer, including all marketing and sales expenses.

Customer Lifetime Value (CLV): The total revenue a business can expect from a single customer throughout their relationship.

Direct Marketing: Direct communication with targeted customers through mail, email, or phone to prompt an action.

Engagement Rate: A metric used to measure the level of interaction with content on social media or other platforms.

Fast-Moving Consumer Goods (FMCG): Products that are sold quickly at relatively low cost, like packaged food, beverages, and toiletries.

Gross Rating Point (GRP): A measure in advertising to indicate the number of exposures to a target audience.

Influencer Marketing: Partnering with influential people to promote products or services.

Key Performance Indicator (KPI): A measurable value that demonstrates how effectively a company is achieving key business objectives.

Market Penetration: The extent to which a product or service is known and/or used by customers in a market.

Net Promoter Score (NPS): A metric measuring the likelihood of customers recommending a company's product or service.

Omnichannel Marketing: A marketing approach providing customers with a fully integrated shopping experience across all channels.

Pay-Per-Click (PPC): An online advertising model where advertisers pay a fee each time one of their ads is clicked.

Return on Investment (ROI): A measure used to evaluate the profitability of an investment.

Search Engine Optimisation (SEO): Increasing the quantity and quality of traffic to a website through organic search engine results.

Segmentation: Dividing a market into distinct groups of buyers with different needs or behaviours.

Unique Selling Proposition (USP): A factor differentiating a product from its competitors, like the lowest cost or highest quality.

Value Proposition: A statement communicating the benefits customers will receive from a product or service.

Affiliate Marketing: A marketing arrangement where an online retailer pays commission for traffic or sales generated from referrals.

Brand Equity: The value a brand adds to a product or service, reflected in consumer perception.

Content Marketing: Creating and distributing valuable, relevant, and consistent content to attract a defined audience.

Cost Per Acquisition (CPA): The total cost of acquiring a new customer, including all marketing and sales costs.

Digital Marketing: The promotion of products or brands through one or more forms of electronic media.

Geo-Targeting: Delivering content or advertisements to a user based on their geographic location.

Guerilla Marketing: Unconventional marketing intended to get maximum results from minimal resources.

Impressions: The number of times an advertisement or content is displayed on a screen.

Integrated Marketing Communications (IMC): Integrating communications functions to ensure consistency across all channels.

Lead Generation: The initiation of consumer interest or inquiry into products or services of a business.

Native Advertising: A form of online advertising that matches the form and function of the platform on which it appears.

Organic Reach: The number of unique users who viewed your content without paid distribution.

Programmatic Advertising: Automated buying and selling of online advertising space.

Rebranding: The process of changing the corporate image of an organization.

Remarketing (or Retargeting): Connecting with visitors to your website who may not have made an immediate purchase or inquiry.

Social Media Optimisation (SMO): Managing and growing an organization's message and online presence through social media networks.

Thought Leadership: Being recognized as an authority in a specialized field and whose expertise is sought and often rewarded.

Viral Marketing: A method of marketing whereby consumers are encouraged to share information about a company's goods or services via the Internet.

Word-of-Mouth Marketing: Oral or written recommendation by a satisfied customer to the prospective customers of a good or service.

A NOTE FROM THE AUTHOR

Thank you for reading "The Marketing Almanac", before you go, I want to leave you with a thought, a call to action, that has been an undercurrent of this journey. It's about disrupting the status quo of marketing operations and shaking up the old ways we see marketing, sales, and business development. The usual approach has them apart, but I believe they're stronger together.

If your workplace keeps these areas separate, here's my take – showing how marketing can be the heartbeat of the organisation, enriching every decision, strategy, and interaction with its insight and creativity could change everything. I am not talking about websites and social media, I am talking about understanding people deeply and bringing that insight into every decision, service, or product you sell.

But if you are hitting a wall trying to bring this change, there might be places that get it, where these teams work as one. These places value new ideas and could be a great fit for you. Before you think about moving on, though, maybe try sharing this book with your bosses or your leadership team. It could spark something. This almanac is about what marketing can do when knit into the fabric of an organisation.

Marketing is always changing, and it thrives on people coming together, sharing ideas, and trying new things. I wrote this book hoping to start conversations and inspire change. And I'm here for all of it - your thoughts, your challenges, your successes. You can reach me at michelle.pontes@gmail.com.

Your willingness to look at things differently is what will push me forward to write next years edition.
Let's keep talking.

All the best,
MP

ABOUT THE AUTHOR

Michelle stands as a testament to persistence, depth, and the adamant courage to step beyond comfort zones. Driven by an inherent belief in pushing boundaries, Michelle has carved her niche, transforming challenges into stepping stones.

Her strength lies in her relentless pursuit of meaning and purpose.

Despite her accomplishments, she remains grounded, often found by the river's side, lost in her own thoughts or a book, with a napkin or a loose piece of paper nearby - waiting to capture her next big idea.

Michelle's approach to life and work is characterised by a unique blend of strategic thinking and creative spontaneity. She has a keen eye for opportunities where others see obstacles. Her independence and self-reliance serve as the cornerstones of her success.

Her book, "The Marketing Almanac," manifests her firm belief in continuous improvement, offering readers a glimpse into the mind of someone who never settles for "good enough."

Printed in Great Britain
by Amazon

40458970R00106